HOW TO

W9-CSB-599

HOW TO WIN OVER WORRY

A Practical Formula for Successful Living

by

John Edmund Haggai

President and Founder of
HAGGAI INSTITUTE
for Advanced Leadership Training

Zondervan Publishing House
Grand Rapids, Michigan

Dedicated to ARNOLD SCHARBAUER OF
   MIDLAND, TEXAS
CARL NEWTON OF SAN ANTONIO, TEXAS
mighty men of valor and cherished friends

Zondervan Publishing House,
1415 Lake Drive, S.E.,
Grand Rapids, Michigan 49506

ISBN 0-310-25712-3

Printed in the United States of America

86   87   88 / 40   39   38   37

CONTENTS

Preface

Our world is sick with sin and paralyzed by fear. In our nation more people are committing suicide each year than are dying from the five most common communicable diseases. While twentieth-century drugs, administered by skilled physicians, have nearly obliterated the ravages and perils of infectious diseases, all manner of psychosomatic illnesses, high blood pressure, hypertension, etc., have become the insignia of our emotionally frustrated and mentally sick society. We have conquered outer space, but the heart of man is still wild and untamed.

Millions of people across our land are saddled with the problem of anxiety, worry, duress — call it what you will. They are beginning to realize what a hazardous problem it is. Having quaffed the intoxicating cup of selfish pleasure and egocentric interests, we are now suffering the hangover of intellectual confusion, emotional perplexity, and volitional paralysis.

The late Adlai E. Stevenson once said, "We have confused the free with the free and easy. We are in danger of becoming slaves to a tyranny more intimate and inescapable than any Stalin or Mao Tse-tung could impose. We can be made slaves simply by the clutter and complexity of modern living — which notoriously leaves no time for serious thought. . . .

"A nation glued to the television screen, one that spends more than any other society has on drink and tranquilizers, one that spends more on advertising than education, that evades the rigors of creative activity and is indifferent to all but athletic excellence, one that enjoys the trivial and the mediocre, one committed to pleasure and profit alone — such a chaotic, selfish, indifferent, commercial society will be at a loss before the 'Iron Pioneers' of the new collective society."

People need help and need it desperately. The worry problem is at the root of much domestic strife, business failure, social injustices, economic crises, seemingly incurable sicknesses, and premature deaths — to mention but a few of its hazards. Much has been said about the problem, but in too many instances the emphasis given has been restricted to diagnosis. We are suffering from the paralysis of analysis. We need prescription. We need the answer in terms easily understood. God's Word offers the needed help in these terms.

About two years ago on the spur of the moment, I felt impressed to change the message I had planned to give at a weekday morning service in one of our crusades. I spoke on the problem of worry. The response staggered me and amazed the other members of the team. Since that time this is one subject I have preached, without exception, in every crusade. The attendance and the response at the services where this subject is presented never cease to overwhelm me. It is not unusual for a large auditorium to be packed on a Saturday night with people who have crowded in to hear God's answer to the problem of worry. Even in our city-wide crusades — sometimes conducted in stadiums — the largest attendance is recorded when this subject is presented. This has indicated to me the overriding concern of a large segment of our population.

Literally hundreds of people have come up after the services or have written later requesting the message in print. At first I thought it was a temporary enthusiasm that soon would be dissipated, but repeated requests have indicated that the concern was genuine and abiding. Thus you have the explanation for this book. This book is the amplification of the message, "How to Win Over Worry," which it has been my privilege to preach from coast to coast.

On my desk is a folder containing solicited testimonials to the use God has made of this message. The following is a sample letter. (Obviously fictitious names are substituted):

> Dear Mr. Haggai:
> When you came to Centerville two weeks ago my life was a miserable mess. I was taking four kinds of medicine, was trying to face giving up managing a $150,000 insurance agency because of "nerves" and my relationship in my family was at a serious state. Now I am fine. Thank you, thank you, thank you.
>
> Sincerely,
> John Doe

It is my earnest prayer that God may use this book to help thousands of people win over worry and enter into that "peace that passeth all understanding."

The interest family counselors, members of mental health societies, psychologists, physicians, and many others have registered with respect to this message has been most gratifying. Their encouragement has spurred and sped the production of this book.

Let it be understood that this volume makes no pretense of being a textbook in psychology or a medical advisor or any other type of technological treatise. In this book is presented the biblical formula for victory over the vicious problem of worry and you will find the formula in complete harmony with the laws of health and psychology.

Literary perfection has not been the chief aim of this book. The message has been poured out of a burning and burdened heart onto a dictaphone belt and transcribed by my secretary. It has been done in snatches — in libraries, in hotel rooms, in my study at home, in private homes, in business offices, and even in airports. Italics within Scripture references are my own.

You will notice that more space is given to the division in

which poise is discussed than to any other. This was done deliberately because this subject has received little or no treatment in the majority of books relating to this problem. You will further notice that the chapter on stewardship is probably the longest chapter in the book. After you read it, you will understand the reason. Acting on the suggestions laid down in this chapter could revolutionize the lives of multiplied thousands of people.

This book is suggestive rather than exhaustive. There are many additional factors in the various divisions of the book I had hoped to discuss, but space limitation ruled it out.

Some will question why an evangelist would produce a book of this type. A few will question that a book such as this has any relationship to evangelism. Let me suggest that the Greek word from which we get the word *evangelize* is translated in the King James Version, almost without exception, "preach the Gospel." Check the Scriptures used in this book along with their relevance to our contemporary needs. You will quickly conclude, I think, that this is a gospel presentation and therefore evangelistic.

Let me earnestly suggest that you read the first three chapters at one sitting. This is necessary if you would get the proper perspective of the material discussed in the remaining chapters.

It is here appropriate to express my profound appreciation to Miss Pauline Utterback, stenographer nonpareil, who typed and proofread the manuscript. She also made many fine and helpful suggestions. Without her assistance this book would not have been completed.

I am also indebted to the assistance given to me by the public libraries in Richmond, Virginia; Lawton, Oklahoma; Petersburg, Virginia; and my home town of Louisville, Kentucky.

My friend, the Rev. Robert F. Martin, pastor of the First Baptist Church of Greenville, Kentucky, suggested the title.

— JOHN EDMUND HAGGAI

Louisville, Kentucky

Part 1

Surveying the Problem

1

Meet Public Enemy Number One

"Died of worry" could be written factually on many tombstones.

In a splendid book entitled *Every Other Bed* written by Mike Gorman, the Executive Director of the National Mental Health Committee, you read the astounding and terrifying fact that every other hospital bed in the United States is occupied by a mentally disturbed person. The book further declares that it is possible even now to foresee a day — not too far off — *when two-thirds of our hospital beds will be occupied by persons with mental illnesses,* and worry is one of the major causes.

Mental illness is costing this country billions of dollars every year.

It is conservatively estimated that many more Americans are committing suicide each year (the result of stress, duress, anxiety, worry) than die from the most common communicable diseases. During 1972, 24,280 people committed suicide! During the same time 5,400 more people committed suicide than the total number who were victims of homicide.

During 1970, 8,070 people died as a result of ulcers of the stomach and duodenum. It is firmly established that worry is the primary factor involved in stomach and duodenal ulcers.

An estimated 17 million Americans are suffering from some form of mental illness. The chances are one in ten that you may be suffering from mental illness right now, and you may not even know it.

In their book, *Social Class and Mental Illness,* Professors August B. Hollingshead and Frederick C. Redlich of Yale University surveyed the nearly quarter of a million residents of New Haven. The results of the survey disclose that 1,891 persons were under psychiatric care.

We were shocked during World War II at the news that one-third of a million of our finest young people were killed in combat. The fact that during the same period over a million civilians died from heart disease — much of it caused by worry — provoked hardly the raising of an eyebrow.

The late Dr. Alexis Carroll said, "Businessmen who don't know how to fight worry, die young."

One of the leading physicians of the nation stated that 70 percent of all patients who go to doctors could cure themselves if they could only get rid of their fears and worries. He himself admitted to having suffered for twelve years with a stomach ulcer from this very cause — worry.

Read *Stop Worrying and Get Well* by Dr. Edward Podolsky, a reputable medical doctor. It deals with the correlation between worry and heart trouble, high blood pressure, some forms of asthma, rheumatism, ulcers, cold, thyroid malfunction, arthritis, migraine headaches, blindness, and a host of stomach disorders in addition to ulcers.

There are some outstanding young doctors who have founded and who staff the Medical Arts Clinic in Corsicana, Texas. Two of these, a brilliant young surgeon by the name of Louis Gibson and a sharp young internist by the name of Robert S. Bone, told me recently that the first complaint of more than 70 percent of the people coming to them is, "Doctor, I can't sleep." Why? Worry!

The very emphasis being given to the problem of worry today is symptomatic of its threat to our nation. For instance, on my desk today are two rather popular magazines. One is

Pageant. The other is *Reader's Digest*. *Pageant* carries an article, "How to Face Your Fears, Tensions, Worries," that covers nearly eleven pages. *Reader's Digest* carries an article, "The Inner Secret of Health," that covers eight and one-half pages.

Several years ago a pastor friend of mine, Eddie Lieberman, was asked to make a visit to try to help a young lady who was depressed and ill. He went to see her. She told him that she was sick, that she didn't love her husband any more (he was overseas in the Armed Forces at that time) and that she wanted a divorce. Physically, she went from bad to worse. Soon she was a paralytic confined to her bed, completely helpless.

Mr. Lieberman is also a psychologist. (In fact, he was invited to become the first case psychologist in one of our leading Baptist hospitals, but declined to pursue the work for which God had called him — the gospel ministry.)

With his background and knowledge he at once sensed that something was drastically wrong with this girl. He requested and received permission to admit her to Duke University Hospital. While she was there, the psychiatrist induced hypnosis. Under hypnosis she confessed she had received a letter from her husband in which he stated he had fallen in love with another girl. He had asked his wife for a divorce. She had concealed these facts from everyone. Nevertheless it had caused her great anxiety and her anxiety brought about this condition of paralysis. In a futile effort to excape a problem, she had set up a compensatory mechanism. Post-hypnotic effects are of short duration. Because she did not want to be helped and since she refused to face the facts, nothing could be done. Today, in her mid-thirties, she should be vivacious, productive, and happy. Instead she is a morose paralytic headed for a premature grave simply because she refuses to cope with this problem of worry.

One of the characteristics of worry is its contagious nature. Several outstanding psychiatrists believe that worry is much more contagious than such infectious diseases as scarlet fever, poliomyelitis, diphtheria, and the like.

Worry is public enemy number one not only because of its devastating effects upon the individuals involved, but also because of the way it ravages society.

To get a little keener insight into the destruction it effects in the individual and in society, consider exactly what we mean by worry. This book proposes to give the biblical solution to this grave problem. The basic text from which the formula is lifted is Philippians 4:4-8:

> Rejoice in the Lord alway: and again I say, Rejoice. Let your moderation be known unto all men. The Lord is at hand. Be careful for nothing; but in everything by prayer and supplication with thanksgiving let your requests be made known unto God.
>
> And the peace of God, which passeth all understanding, shall keep your hearts and minds through Christ Jesus.
>
> Finally, brethren, whatsoever things are true, whatsoever things are honest, whatsoever things are pure, whatsoever things are lovely, whatsoever things are of good report; if there be any virtue, and if there be any praise, think on these things.

Now read this same passage in the stimulating *Amplified New Testament* translation:

> Rejoice in the Lord always — delight, gladden yourselves in Him; again I say, Rejoice! [Ps. 37:4] Let all men know and perceive and recognize your unselfishness — your considerateness, your forbearing spirit. The Lord is near — He is coming soon. Do not fret or have any anxiety about anything, but in every circumstance and in everything by prayer and petition [definite requests] with thanksgiving continue to make your wants known to God. And God's peace [be yours, that tranquil state of a soul assured of its salvation through Christ, and so fearing nothing from God and content with its earthly lot of whatever sort that is, that peace] which transcends all understanding, shall garrison and mount guard over your hearts and minds in Christ Jesus. For the rest, brethren, whatever is true, whatever is worthy of reverence and is honorable and seemly, whatever is just, whatever is pure, whatever is lovely and lovable, whatever is kind and

winsome and gracious, if there is any virtue and excellence,
if there is anything worthy of praise, think on and weigh and
take account of these things — fix your minds on them.

(Philippians 4:4-8)

The formula for victory over the dread condition of worry
will be revealed in Chapter 3.

The New Testament word for worry is translated "take
thought" and "be careful" in the Authorized Version. J. B.
Phillips correctly translates it "worry."

The word *worry* comes from the Greek word *merimnao*
which is a combination of two words: *merizo* meaning "to
divide" and *nous* meaning "mind" (including the faculties
of perceiving, understanding, feeling, judging, determin-
ing).

Worry, then, means "to divide the mind." Worry divides
the mind between worthwhile interests and damaging
thoughts.

The Apostle James states the unhappy condition of the
person with the divided mind. "A double-minded man is
unstable in all his ways" (James 1:8).

Notice that James says that the man with the divided mind
is unstable in *all his ways*. He is unstable in his emotions.
He is unstable in his thought processes. He is unstable in his
decisions. He is unstable in his judgments.

Peace of mind requires singleness of mind. The worrier
robs himself of peace of mind by dividing his mind.

Worry divides the feelings, therefore the emotions lack
stability.

Worry divides the understanding, therefore convictions
are shallow and changeable.

Worry divides the faculty of perception, therefore observa-
tions are faulty and even false.

Worry divides the faculty of judging, therefore attitudes
and decisions are often unjust. These decisions lead to damage and grief.

Worry divides the determinative faculty, therefore plans

and purposes, if not "scrapped" altogether, are not fulfilled with persistence.

Worry in the extreme leads to *abulia* — "loss of the power to will." Why? The mind is so divided it cannot act in one channel. It is like the mule who stood between two haystacks and starved to death trying to decide from which stack to eat.

Abulia is often termed a nervous breakdown. In such a breakdown pressures have so built up as a result of divided-mindedness that the victim ceases struggling with his problems and responds in a depressed and passive manner.

Worry is the cause of heartbreak, failure, misunderstanding, suspicion, and most unhappiness.

Most homes which have gone on the rocks can point to "the divided mind" as the cause. It may be that the mind was divided between the wife and another woman. It may be that the wife divided her mind between the husband and "mama." Her mind may have been divided between an inexcusably possessive preoccupation with her children and her God-ordained responsibilities to her husband. It may be that the mind was divided between home responsibilities and selfish, personal desires. It may be that the husband divided his mind between an inordinate ambition to succeed and his responsibilities as husband and father. With just a little thought you can come readily to many other possibilities — or certainties — which have divided the mind and wrecked the home.

Who can determine the percentage of school failures effectuated by "the divided mind"? The sons of clergymen, for example, confront difficulties in their youth. That goes for clergymen's daughters as well. If they are model children, the parents of other children hold them up as a pattern of behavior with a result that their fellows detest them. If, on the other hand, they are normally mischievous, the other children appreciate them and their parents detest them. I have a brother who was so sensitive to the fact that he was a minister's son that he deliberately made poor grades so the kids wouldn't think him a "goody-goody." Worry ruined his grades. He has an excellent mind. This fact has since been proven by his collegiate scholastic records. He graduated with honors in a difficult field from one of the nation's leading universities.

Do not some children fail in school because of discord in the home — discord that divides their minds between their scholastic responsibilities and the possible outcome of the domestic cold war? Do not some children bungle their school opportunities simply because they are neglected at home? They feel unwanted and therefore they raise Cain at school to get the attention they do not get at home.

Only the Lord knows how many businesses have been torpedoed by worry — the divided mind. There was a man who opened a hot dog stand. His business grew. He expanded. Soon he had a chain of stands. He was making fabulous money. He sent his son to college. The son graduated with a major in Business Administration. This was in 1933. The father took him into the business. The son said, "You know, Dad, there's a depression on. Business is bad everywhere. Many businesses have gone into bankruptcy. We must be careful. Let's cut down our inventory, reduce our advertising budget, lay off some of the help, and tighten our belts." The father listened to his learned son and followed the advice reluctantly. Yes, you've guessed it. The son succeeded in dividing his father's mind between the principles of success and the potential threats of the depression. Soon their business folded. Worse yet, the father, depressed by the financial reverses, lost his sparkle, his drive, his optimistic outlook with the result that he began to deteriorate physically.

One of the best known tycoons of our nation during this century made and then lost three huge fortunes. Why? Because over and over again he divided his mind between his business interests and gold-digging paramours.

One of the most bitter and cynical men I have ever known was a man loaded with talent. He had more ability than six average men. He could have been a leading cartoonist, a topnotch photographer, a highly paid after-dinner speaker, a humorist, a prosperous realtor, a topflight hotel executive, or a celebrated writer. He never amounted to anything. He saw men who obviously did not possess one fraction of his ability soar to the heights of success while he groveled in the mud. Those who knew him well understood the reason. It was a divided mind. He never came to the point at which he determined what he was going to do. He could not say with Paul the Apostle, ''This one thing I do.'' He would never throw all of his energies in a single project. He aimed at nothing, hit a bull's eye, and then brooded over the result. He became critical of others who did achieve. With a cynicism unparalleled he would rationalize his failure and deal out misery to all of his associates. His health broke completely. A distraught mind inevitably leads to a deteriorated body.

Worry is public enemy number one. It is slaying tens of thousands. It is assaulting great businesses and leaving them a shambles. An emotional tornado, it is ravaging homes, leaving in its wake bitter and frustrated parents, as well as insecure and terrified children — all candidates for psychiatric care.

The biography of multiplied thousands of Americans could well be *Hurry, Worry, and Bury*.

In our nation over the past 100 years the population has increased 671 percent. But during the same time the number of institutionalized mental patients has increased 23,328 percent!

Now please turn to the next chapter. In Chapter 2 we will discuss some of the various ways worriers try to cope with their problem.

2

Throw Away Your Popgun

A popgun is a fine toy for children. It gives them action and noise. It arrests their attention — for a time, at least. When a boy arrives at the age of adolescence, he no longer finds much interest in a popgun. And could there be anything more ludicrous and incongruous than a full-grown man whiling away his time shooting a little dime store popgun?

You cannot kill a bear nor a lion nor any vicious enemy of human life with a popgun. Men do not go hunting with popguns. Nor are soldiers equipped with popguns when called upon to fight an enemy.

Shooting a popgun probably takes as much effort as shooting a twenty-two caliber rifle or many other types of guns. Some popguns make as much noise as real guns. Apart from occupying the attention for a little while, making some noise, and requiring the exertion of some effort, popguns accomplish nothing.

The majority of worriers try to kill this vicious enemy, worry, with popguns. Figuratively speaking, that is. Let us mention a few of the more prominent popguns that are used.

There is the popgun of *flattery*. Flattery is a device used by many seeking to compensate for worry. By flattery the worrier endeavors to secure loyal friends in large numbers. He thereby seeks to immunize himself from danger by building around himself this wall of friends. It is his thought that there is safety in numbers. He reasons that if the dreadful probabilities he fears become calamitous certainties, he will be shielded by this wall of friends.

Obviously flattery accomplishes nothing except to give a temporary and a false security to the flatterer. The very dishonesty of this attempt ultimately adds to the worries of the worrier.

Flattery is mentioned and denounced over thirty times in the Word of God. Job says:

> He that speaketh flattery to his friends, even the eyes of his children shall fail.   (Job 17:5)

Again in Job:

> Let me not, I pray you, accept any man's person, neither let me give flattering titles unto man.
> For I know not to give flattering titles; in so doing my maker would soon take me away.   (Job 32:21,22)

The psalmist scores the sinfulness and foolishness of flattery in Psalm 5:9:

> For there is no faithfulness in their mouth; . . . they flatter with their tongue.

You remember the statement made in the previous chapter that worry is essentially divided-mindedness. Notice now how that fits in with the words of the psalmist in the following words:

> They speak vanity every one with his neighbor: with flattering lips and with a *double heart* do they speak.
>
> (Psalm 12:2)

The wisest man of history, Solomon, admonishes us:

> He that goeth about as a talebearer revealeth secrets: therefore meddle not with him that flattereth with his lips.
>
> (Proverbs 20:19)
>
> A lying tongue hateth those that are afflicted by it; and a flattering mouth worketh ruin.   (Proverbs 26:28)

Another popgun utilized by many worriers is that of *criticism*. Psychologists tell us there are three reasons for this. First, we criticize to elevate ourselves. Second, we criticize to project our miserableness. Third, we criticize the very thing of which we are guilty, or the thing which tempts us and troubles us the most.

No matter what may be your motive for criticism, the old saying is true, "It doesn't take much size to criticize."

Remember that popguns are used only by children and the popgun of criticism, like the other figurative popguns mentioned in this chapter, is used by the most immature personalities.

Worriers often resort to criticism to project their own miserableness. They are miserable and they want everyone else to be miserable. This obviously is not the answer to worry. In thus projecting their own misery people succeed temporarily in getting their minds off their own problems. The tragic result, however, is that the relief is only temporary. In criticizing they are focusing their minds upon negative thoughts and the mischief that inevitably follows negative thinking but adds to their worries. Consequently the depression becomes more intense.

It is true that "what Peter says about Paul tells more about Peter than it does about Paul." Or, in the words of the little couplet:

"Things that thou dost in others see,
are the most prevalent in thee."

The Bible tells us, "To the impure, all are impure." That can be carried out. To the dishonest, all are dishonest. To the untrue, all are untrue. When the worrier criticizes others, he certainly solves none of his own worries. He focuses his attention upon the miserable traits he sees in others which mirror his own condition. His mind is riveted to this destructively negative thinking in such a way that more fear-producing thoughts are bred to add to his already overstocked supply of fears.

Paul the Apostle scores the sin of criticism when in Romans 2:1 he says:

> Therefore thou art inexcusable, O man, whosoever thou
> art that judgest: for wherein thou judgest another, thou con-
> demnest thyself; for thou that judgest doest the same things.

What the worrier fails to realize is that in criticizing others he
is revealing to the world what he himself is.

Another popgun that many worriers use in their endeavor
to kill this vicious enemy of worry is that of *excessive activity*. This is only a temporary escape. Through this means they
try in vain to conquer their worries, but they only postpone
their misery with a temporary emotional intoxication. They
think they are busy when they are only "nervous." (Later on
you will understand why I put the word "nervous" in
quotes.) They are like a worm on a hot rock. As one TV
personality said not too long ago, "They are as nervous as a
long-tailed cat in a room full of rocking chairs." Spinning
their wheels, they are going nowhere. They seem to have
become infatuated with the twentieth-century beatitude,
"Blessed are they that go around in circles, for they shall be
called big wheels."

This feverish activity, motivated by the desire to escape
rather than the urge to produce, solves no problems. It simply
takes the mind for a brief spell off the fear-producing
thoughts that cause the anxiety. This type of activity, instead
of solving problems, actually produces more problems and
thereby intensifies the problem over which victory is sought.

It is amazing how few people can stand their company for
thirty minutes without any action or device such as TV,
radio, books, or any other prop. They do not know the
meaning of the words of our Lord,

> Come ye yourselves apart into a desert place, and rest a
> while: . . .   (Mark 6:31)

They take phenobarbital to go to sleep, dexedrine to get
started in the morning, and they stay tanked up on coffee to
make it through the day. That which they call fervor is
actually no more than emotional fever.

Another popgun used by many worriers in their vain effort

to kill this vicious enemy of worry is the popgun of a *self-righteous resignation*. There is nothing righteous about this kind of resignation. You notice I said it is a self-righteous resignation. They will assert, "My cross is heavy, but I am determined to take it valiantly." This is almost blasphemous. Wherever the biblical injunction, "take up thy cross," appears, it is referring to death to sin and death to self. This is the exact antithesis of the attitude just referred to. The Bible never refers to any problem, grief, dilemma as a cross that some are called to bear. The man who really bears his cross is the man who knows no worry. He has died to sin and to self. Thus he is invulnerable to destructive fears. He has peace because his mind is ever staid upon Christ and because he trusts in Christ.

Jesus never complained about the weight of His cross. However, He bore a cross. A real cross — a cross for you and for me.

Our Lord's disciples rejoiced that "they were counted worthy to suffer shame for His name" (Acts 5:41).

These people who respond to worry, fear and anxiety with a self-righteous resignation say one thing, but they live another. They delude no one but themselves. Although they claim to want to bring glory to God, their faces would "draw a wart" on a tombstone. They repeat the sin of Jonah who said in Jonah 4:3:

> Therefore now, O Lord, take, I beseech thee, my life from me; for it is better for me to die than to live.

And the sin of Elijah:

> . . . It is enough; now, O Lord, take away my life; for I am not better than my fathers. (1 Kings 19:4c)

This is not spiritual courage. This is disgusting cowardice. It is the most revolting type of self-pity.

Some worriers resort to the popgun of *alcohol* and/or *narcotics* in a vain effort to kill the vicious enemy of worry. This gives them temporary exhilaration during which their minds may not be focused upon the fear-producing thoughts that cause them so much grief. However, this type of behavior only postpones the problem. It ultimately increases the agony.

Perspective is distorted under the influence of stimulants. This often leads to regrettable circumstances which result in an increase of the problems of the worrier. Who can calculate the damage done by the many plays (whether in book form, staged on Broadway, projected on the television or movie screen) which portray the unrequited lover desperately going down to the corner saloon to drink away his sorrows. The attitude that a drunken spree is the way to escape an agonizing situation produces pernicious results. The Japanese say: "A man takes a drink, then the drink takes a drink, and the next drink takes the man."

Solomon, the sage of the ages, speaks wisely when he says:

> Who hath woe? who hath sorrow? who hath contentions? who hath babbling? who hath wounds without cause? who hath redness of eyes?
> They that tarry long at the wine; they that go to seek mixed wine.   (Proverbs 23:29,30)

It is still true that:

> Wine is a mocker, strong drink is raging: and whosoever is deceived thereby is not wise.   (Proverbs 20:1)

Some worriers resort to yet another popgun. They seek to conquer worry by *positive thinking*. Now positive thinking is good. Certainly a person cannot have positive thoughts and fear-producing, worrisome thoughts at the same time. Nevertheless, the worrier needs help from outside — or to be more specific, from above. It is one thing to know what we ought to do. It is another thing to have the ability to do it. The Ten Commandments showed man what he must be and what he must do, but no man — our own Lord, the God-man excepted — has ever kept the Ten Commandments. It is one thing to know what we must be and what we must do, and another to meet the demands.

With all of my heart I believe in the power of positive thinking. Let it be understood, however, that God alone is the source of positive thoughts. Paul says in 2 Timothy 1:7:

> For God hath not given us the spirit of fear; but of power, and of love, and of a sound mind.

Positive thoughts do not constitute a useless "popgun" in this instance. Rather they produce the erroneous concept that man in his own strength can bring about the kind of mental attitude that will banish fear and worry. Man might just as well try to shoot an African lion with a popgun as to conquer his worry with his own self-inspired and self-produced positive attitude.

Later on in the book you will notice that much emphasis is given to positive thinking. Equal emphasis is also made on the basis of human experience and on the basis of God's Word that there is no such thing as peace except to those who have properly related themselves to the Lord Jesus Christ, the Prince of Peace. Apart from divine help a proper mental attitude — one that gives peace — is totally impossible. A man's belief that he can be the source of a proper mental attitude is a Pollyanna notion that leads ultimately to frustration.

There are many other "popguns" used to slay the deadly beast, the enemy worry. Those who resort to the use of these various popguns reveal their immaturity and their helplessness. I do not say this disparagingly. God grant that this book will lead them to a proper relationship with God through Christ who is our Peace (cf. Ephesians 2:14). The first requisite for help must be that you *throw away your popgun*.

Thousands of people every year resort to the popgun of *suicide*. It goes without saying this accomplishes nothing. It is like a man cutting off his head to cure the headache.

One of the most heart-rending articles I've ever read appeared on the front page of the May 21, 1931 edition of the *New York Times*. This article dealt with the suicide of Ralph Barton. Mr. Barton was an outstanding cartoonist, one of the nation's leading caricaturists. He was highly gifted, a great writer. His life ended tragically by his own hand.

In his suicide note he told about the melancholia he had

been suffering. Apparently his fears nearly drove him mad. Read verbatim part of what he said in his suicide note:

> It (melancholia) has prevented my getting anything like the full value out of my talent, and the past three years has made work a torture to do at all. It has made it impossible for me to enjoy the simple pleasures of life.

Now I am taking the liberty of italicizing that part of his note which I want impressed upon you.

> *I have run from wife to wife, from house to house, and from country to country in a ridiculous effort to escape from myself.* In doing so I am very much afraid that I have brought a great deal of unhappiness to those who have loved me . . .
> *No one thing is responsible for this and no one person — except myself* . . .
> *I did it because I am fed up with inventing devices for getting through the twenty-four hours a day and with bridging over a few months periodically with some beautiful interest,* such as a new gal who annoyed me to the point where I forgot my own troubles.

Poor fellow. Brilliant of mind! How tragic that a life such as his, filled with great possibilities for blessing his generation in the will of God, had to end in such tragedy!

He tried to kill the stalking lion of worry and melancholia with a series of useless popguns.

Throw away your popgun. This is your first step if you would conquer worry.

Toward the end of Chapter 3 the biblical formula for winning over worry will be disclosed.

3

Worry Is A Sin

Worry is a SIN — a blighting sin that has become the subject matter of nonsensical satire.

Worry cannot be excused as an uncontrollable condition. It is a sin for two reasons: (1) Worry is distrust in the truthfulness of God and (2) worry is detrimental to the temple of God.

(1) Worry is distrust in the truthfulness of God.

When you worry you accuse God of falsehood.

God's Word says, "And we know that all things work together for good to them that love God, to them who are the called according to his purpose" (Romans 8:28).

>Worry says, "Thou liest, O God!"

God's Word says, "He hath done all things well" (Mark 7:37).

>Worry says, "Thou liest, O God!"

God's Word says, "I can do all things through Christ which strengtheneth me" (Philippians 4:13).

>Worry says, "Thou liest, O God!"

God's Word says, "But my God shall supply all your need according to his riches in glory by Christ Jesus" (Philippians 4:19).

Worry says, "Thou liest, O God!"

God's Word says, "I will never leave thee, nor forsake thee" (Hebrews 13:5).

Worry says, "Thou liest, O God!"

God's Word says, "He careth for you" (1 Peter 5:7).

Worry says, "Thou liest, O God!"

God's Word says, "Take no thought for your life, what ye shall eat, or what ye shall drink; nor yet for your body, what ye shall put on . . . .for your heavenly Father knoweth that ye have need of all these things" (Matthew 6:25a,32b).

Worry says, "Thou liest, O God!"

Worry is hypocrisy, for it professes faith in God and at the same time assails the reality of His truthfulness.

If it is highly insulting to call a man a liar (although the fact is that David probably spoke the truth when he said, "All men are liars"), how infinitely more inexcusable it is to accuse the sovereign God of falsehood. He is the God "who cannot lie."

> In hope of eternal life, which God, that cannot lie, promised before the world began.   (Titus 1:2)
>
> He that believeth not God hath made him a liar; . . .
>   (1 John 5:10)

(2) Worry is a sin because it is detrimental to the temple of God.

If a group of vandals should crash into your church some dark night and succeed in shattering the stained-glass windows, ripping up the carpeting, smashing the furniture, wrecking the musical instruments, disfiguring the walls, and ravaging the Sunday school rooms, you would react with justifiable anger and prosecute them to the full extent of the law. The laws of the land provide stringent penalties for disturbance of public worship and for destruction of church property. You would make the most of these laws, as well you should.

Yet worry is a far more inexcusable and grievous sin than this vandalism of church property. In all probability, these vandals were not professing Christians, while many who worry are. Furthermore, there is no inherent value in a church building. True, it symbolizes worship. It symbolizes the work and the Word of God. However, its only inherent value is symbolic. God does not dwell in the church building as such. He dwells there only as He dwells in the hearts of those who worship there.

God *does* dwell in the heart of every believer.

> Know ye not that ye are the temple of God, and that the Spirit of God dwelleth in you?   (1 Corinthians 3:16)

> What? know ye not that your body is the temple of the Holy Ghost which is in you, which ye have of God, and ye are not your own?   (1 Corinthians 6:19)

> Ye also, as lively stones, are built up a spiritual house, an holy priesthood, to offer up spiritual sacrifices, acceptable to God by Jesus Christ.   (1 Peter 2:5)

> And because ye are sons, God hath sent forth the Spirit of his Son into your hearts . . .   (Galatians 4:6)

Worry debilitates and even destroys the temple of God which is *your own body*, Christian! In Chapter 1 we mentioned some of the detrimental effects worry has on the body — God's temple. Let's review for a moment. Some of the ailments caused by worry are heart trouble, high blood pressure, some forms of asthma, rheumatism, ulcers, colds, thyroid malfunction, arthritis, migraine headaches, blindness, and a host of stomach disorders apart from ulcers. It also causes palpitations, pains in the back of the neck, indigestion, nausea, constipation, diarrhea, dizziness, unexplainable fatigue, insomnia, allergies and temporary paralysis.

Many other reasons could be given to substantiate the fact that worry is a sin.

Worry is a sin because it is symptomatic of prayerlessness.

> Moreover as for me, God forbid that I should sin against the Lord in ceasing to pray for you. . . . (1 Samuel 12:23)

No one can pray and worry at the same time.

> Thou wilt keep him in perfect peace, whose mind is stayed on thee: because he trusteth in thee.   (Isaiah 26:3)

When you pray your mind is staid on Christ and you have His
assurance of perfect peace. Worry is therefore banished.

Worry is a sin because of what it does to family life.

> Wives, submit yourselves unto your own husbands, as
> unto the Lord.
>
> Husbands, love your wives, even as Christ also loved the
> church, and gave himself for it.
>
> Nevertheless let every one of you in particular so love his
> wife even as himself; and the wife see that she reverence her
> husband.   (Ephesians 5:22,25,33)

These injunctions in the book of Ephesians are violated
and disobeyed when worry is in the saddle.

Worry is a sin because it undermines our Christian witness. In Matthew 5:16 Jesus says:

> Let your light so shine before men, that they may see your
> good works, and glorify your Father which is in heaven.

Someone may say, "Oh, yes, Mr. Haggai, you can talk
like that in an overly confident, pedantic manner. You are
young and enjoy good health, but you don't know what I have
to put up with."

Let me say, friend, that I too hold the distinction of having
suffered a "nervous breakdown." The reason I put the words
"nervous breakdown" in quotes is that most so-called nervous breakdowns do not originate with any organic problem in
the nervous system. Actually, most of that that goes under the
label "nervousness" ought to be called mental maladjust-
ment.

When I was twenty-four years old and pastor of my first
church, I suffered one of these so-called "nervous breakdowns" which was but the culmination of stress, anxiety,
worry. I was full-time pastor of a church, taking nineteen
college hours, and conducting evangelistic campaigns. My
wife felt sorry for me. My church felt sorry for me. My doctor
felt sorry for me. But no one felt as sorry for me as I felt for
myself. Finally the doctor ordered me to get away for several
weeks of rest and diversion. My church graciously made this
possible.

During those weeks of convalescence God spoke to my heart and showed me that my condition was not the result of any organic difficulty, but the result of the *sin* of worry. With gratitude to God I can say that since the fall of 1948 I have not lost five minutes of sleep over any problem, difficulty, tension, worry, or any adverse circumstance of life whatsoever. Today my physical condition is as perfect as can be. In fact, an insurance company returned to me the culmination of seven years of penalties I had been paying on premiums because of a condition in my twenties which they feared. I attribute the improved physical condition to the conquest of worry.

Worry is a sin. The Bible is the only book that deals adequately with the problem of sin. Quite logically, then, we go to the Word of God to find the solution to this problem.

> Rejoice in the Lord alway: and again I say, Rejoice.
>
> Let your moderation be known unto all men. The Lord is at hand.
>
> Be careful for nothing; but in every thing by prayer and supplication with thanksgiving let your requests be made known unto God.
>
> And the peace of God, which passeth all understanding, shall keep your hearts and minds through Christ Jesus.
>
> Finally, brethren, whatsoever things are true, whatsoever things are honest, whatsoever things are just, whatsoever things are pure, whatsoever things are lovely, whatsoever things are of good report; if there be any virtue, and if there be any praise, think on these things.   (Philippians 4:4-8)
>
> Delight yourselves in the Lord, yes, find your joy in him at all times. Have a reputation for gentleness, and never forget the nearness of your Lord.
>
> Don't worry over anything whatever; tell God every detail of your needs in earnest and thankful prayer, and the peace of God, which transcends human understanding, will keep constant guard over your hearts and minds as they rest in Christ Jesus.
>
> My brothers I need only add this. If you believe in goodness and if you value the approval of God, fix your minds on whatever is true and honourable and just and pure and lovely

and admirable.   (Philippians 4:4-8 — Phillips)

Now give thought to the words of our Lord in Matthew 6:25-34:

> Therefore I tell you, stop being perpetually uneasy (anxious and worried) about your life, what you shall eat or what you shall drink, and about your body, what you shall put on. Is not life greater (in quality) than food, and the body (far above and more excellent) than clothing? Look at the birds of the air; they neither sow nor reap nor gather into barns, and yet your heavenly Father keeps feeding them. Are you not worth more than they? And which of you by worrying and being anxious can add one unit of measure (cubit) to his stature or to the span of his life? (Ps. 39:5-7). And why should you be anxious about clothes? Consider the lilies of the field and learn thoroughly how they grow; they neither toil nor spin; Yet I tell you, even Solomon in all his magnificence (excellence, dignity and grace) was not arrayed like one of these (1 Kings 10:4-7) But if God so clothes the grass of the field, which today is alive and green and tomorrow is tossed into the furnace, will He not much more surely clothe you, O you men with little faith?
>
> Therefore do not worry and be anxious, saying, What are we going to have to eat? or, What are we going to have to drink? or, What are we going to have to wear? For the Gentiles (heathen) wish for and crave and diligently seek after all these things; and your heavenly Father well knows that you need them all. But seek for (aim at and strive after) first of all His kingdom, and His righteousness (His way of doing and being right), and then all these things taken together will be given you besides.
>
> So do not worry or be anxious about tomorrow, for tomorrow will have worries and anxieties of its own. Sufficient for each day is its own trouble.
>
>   (Matthew 6:25-34 — *Amplified New Testament*)

The passage in Philippians 4:4-8 constitutes the biblical basis for this book. Out of these verses the thesis of this book is lifted. As we progress, other Scriptures will be used to give added emphasis, insights, illustrations.

Now here is the formula for victory over worry:

PRAISE *plus* POISE *plus* PRAYER *equals* PEACE

Subsequent chapters will amplify and develop this formula found in Philippians 4. The factors involved in praise and in poise and in prayer will be discussed. Suggestions — specific suggestions — will be made for the purpose of assisting you in putting this formula into practice.

Observance of this formula would sweeten the atmosphere of many homes, convert many a faltering business into a thriving success, significantly improve the scholastic level of many a student, give meaning and purpose to many an aimless life, and deliver many a person from a premature grave by curing what is now psychosomatic illness (that is, a physical disorder originating in or aggravated by emotional turbulence) but which would if left alone, deteriorate into organic illness.

Remember the formula: Praise Plus Poise Plus Prayer Equals Peace. Write this formula in large letters. Place one on the mirror of your medicine cabinet where you shave or on the mirror of your dresser. It will be well for the husband to place one in a conspicuous place in the office where he works and for the housewife to have one placed over the sink or in some prominent place where it will catch her eye during the daytime. It will also be well if you will attach one to the sun visor in your automobile. You will find great profit if you will place this formula in several conspicuous places where it will command your attention several times during the day.

Let me further suggest that you memorize the verses found in Philippians 4:4-8. It will be helpful for you to repeat them aloud every morning and every night until they become a part of you.

Now you are ready to turn to Chapter 4 as we begin the discussion of the cure of this vicious sin, worry.

Part 2
Praise

4

The Requirement
to Rejoice

Rejoice evermore. (1 Thessalonians 5:16)

Rejoice in the Lord alway: and again I say, Rejoice.
(Philippians 4:4)

Delight yourselves in the Lord, yes, find your joy in him at all times. (Philippians 4:4 — Phillips)

You say, "But I don't feel like rejoicing. I don't feel like being happy." By that you mean that the circumstances engulfing you are not such as contribute to your happiness.

The majority of people who are chronic worriers make the ridiculous mistake of waiting until the circumstances engulfing them change. You must change the circumstances whenever possible.

Happiness is not a state of becoming. It is a state of being. You don't acquire happiness. You assume happiness.

Notice that the verse (Philippians 4:4) is in the imperative mood. It is mandatory. Paul doesn't say, "If you are so disposed let me suggest that you rejoice." No. He says, "Rejoice in the Lord alway: and again I say, Rejoice." Literally it could be translated, "Keep on rejoicing in the Lord always: and again I say, keep on rejoicing." Make the joy of the Lord the habit pattern of your life. When you fail to do this, you sin.

You rejoice when you praise. You cannot praise God without rejoicing in God and rejoicing in the circumstances, no matter how unpleasant, which God permits.

The word *praise* in its various forms, and the word *rejoice* in its various forms, are mentioned more than 550 times in the Word of God. The very fact that this subject receives such repetitious attention in the Book of God indicates its importance.

In Psalm 34:1 David said:

> I will bless the Lord at all times: his praise shall continually be in my mouth.

Praise was the habit pattern of David's life even though, like you, David had many troubles and difficulties. He often passed through deep waters. One son, Adonijah, broke his heart. Absalom, another son, betrayed his father and tried to usurp his authority. Another son, Ammon, brought grief to David's heart when he committed adultery with his half sister, Tamar. You also remember how viciously Shimei cursed David on one occasion. Every Sunday school pupil remembers the story of Saul's persecution of David. Saul repeatedly sought David's life and with barbaric treachery hounded him. Yet in all of this David blessed the Lord and fulfilled the requirement to rejoice. God's praise was continually in David's mouth.

In Psalm 33:1 David admonishes us to

> Rejoice in the Lord, O ye righteous: for praise is comely for the upright.

This is the injunction of the man who was "a man after God's own heart."

After Peter and the apostles had been beaten mercilessly for speaking "in the name of Jesus," they departed, "rejoicing that they were counted worthy to suffer shame for his name" (Acts 5:41).

You are entitled to no particular commendation simply because you rejoice when everything goes well. When, however, you have made praise and rejoicing the habit pattern of your life you have arrived at that place where you not only bring glory to God, but you set up an immunity against worry.

Rejoice even on blue Mondays and black Fridays.

Though it seems that friends have betrayed you, neighbors are vicious and mean to you, relatives don't appreciate you and tragedy overtakes you, you will conquer worry with the attitude expressed in Isaiah 12:2,4:

> Behold, God is my salvation; I will trust, and not be afraid: for the Lord JEHOVAH is my strength and my song; he also is become my salvation.
>
> And in that day shall ye say, Praise the Lord, call upon his name, declare his doings among the people, make mention that his name is exalted.

Mr. Owen Cooper of Yazoo City, Mississippi, is one of the nation's outstanding Christian laymen and one of a Mississippi's top-ranking citizens. Sometime ago his beautiful home, representing the dreams and hard work of many years, went up in smoke. Some of the members of the family barely escaped with their lives. The fire completely gutted the home and destroyed nearly everything of value.

Shortly after the terrible fire, Mr. Cooper's pastor, Dr. Harold Shirley, told me that the entire family was in prayer meeting the following night. In that service Mr. Cooper arose during the testimony time and with a radiance that only God can give expressed his gratitude to the Lord for sparing their lives. He had learned years before the truth of Romans 8:28:

> And we know that all things work together for good to them that love God, to them who are the called according to his purpose.

Despite this calamity, the habit pattern of the Cooper family could not be affected adversely.

Remember what has been said previously. There is no condition or circumstance that can justify worry. Worry is a sin. Praise is an antidote to worry.

One of the most radiant Christian men I have ever met passed through a heart-crushing trial several years ago. To help augment the family income during the depression, he

and his wife provided room and board for a "highly respected
citizen." The man whom they took in turned out to be a
Judas, a betrayer. He seduced my friend's wife with diaboli-
cal cunning. When she tried to break off the relationship he
went beserk. He strangled her and then put her baby in the
oven and turned on the gas, murdering the little one by
asphyxiation. He the took the couple's eight-year-old son out
into the garage and strangled him with a piece of wire. Then
the depraved man returned to the kitchen, lay down on some
chairs in front of the stove, with all the gas jets on.

The rescue squad was able to revive the insane murderer.
But my friend lost his wife and children in one terrible series
of tragedies.

This crushing blow would have upset the mental balance of
a lesser man than my radiant Christian friend. In the strength
of the Lord he actually went to the penitentiary to witness to
the murderer of his entire family. The way my friend conducted himself through that ordeal and during the subsequent
years has had an impact for good and for God that words
cannot express. Of course he was grief-stricken. But through
it all the joy of the Lord remained his abiding and unwavering
possession.

You say you have troubles? Surely you do. We all have.
When rejoicing has become the habit pattern of your life you
are not a thermometer personality registering the temperature
of your environment. You are rather a thermostat personality
setting the temperature. You have learned, in the words of
Paul to "Rejoice evermore" (1 Thessalonians 5:16).

Paul was no "ivory tower theorist." He urged the Christians at Philippi to "Rejoice in the Lord alway: and again I
say, Rejoice" (Philippians 4:4). He was a prisoner in Rome.
He did not say, "Cry with me," or "Mourn with me," but
"Rejoice with me." What an hysterical time he could have
had, waiting to be martyred. If he could rejoice in an hour like
that, what excuse can we find for our anxieties?

To help you obey this commandment — obedience to
which will revolutionize your life — let me suggest some
helps. Please turn to Chapter 5 for the first suggested help.

5

How to Control
Your Feelings

Think and act joyfully and you will feel joyful. You can control your feelings by controlling your thoughts and your actions.

It is a basic law of psychology that you will feel as you act or think. In other words, if you don't feel the way you want to feel, think and act the way you ought to feel, and soon you will feel the way you are thinking and acting — ideally this will be the way God wants you to feel. I will give you an illustration. Go to a quiet room, stand with your feet about a foot apart at the heels and at forty-five degree angles. Clasp your hands behind your back, letting them hang loosely. Bow your back and neck and head slightly, maintaining complete relaxation of the body. Now start thinking resentful thoughts.

Did you observe what happened? Immediately you straightened up because of the contraction of your muscles. You became taut. Your thoughts, actions, and feelings are interrelated.

When a man comes into my study and sits down in a relaxed manner, placing the ankle of his right leg loosely over the knee of his left leg and leans back, I know he has absolute confidence in me. He has no fear of me, for a position of defense would be hard to assume from this posture.

Carry this over into your everyday life. When you are depressed and forlorn and feel that you have nothing but trouble, *smile*. *Throw your shoulders back*. *Take a good deep breath*. *Sing*. Better still, *force yourself to laugh*. Keep forcing it until you are laughing heartily. At first it will seem mockery, but I guarantee you, it will chase away your gloom.

You cannot think *fear* and act *courageously*. Conversely, you cannot think *courage* and act *fearfully*. You cannot think *hatred* and act *kindly*. Conversely, you cannot think *kindly* and act *hatefully*. Your feelings inevitably correspond to your dominant thoughts and actions.

Is this scriptural? Absolutely! God's Word says, "For as he thinketh in his heart so is he" (Proverbs 23:7).

Now once again read verse eight of our text and see how important it is.

> Finally, brethren, whatsoever things are true, whatsoever things are honest, whatsoever things are just, whatsoever things are pure, whatsoever things are lovely, whatsoever things are of good report; if there be any virtue, and if there be any praise, think on these things. (Philippians 4:8)

Obedience to the command of verse eight will result in obedience to the command of verse four. As you think, so will you feel. Our feelings are revealed by our actions. For instance, when I see a man with his feet set at ten minutes to two and his lips at twenty past eight, who pushes his weight instead of carrying it, I say to myself, "Watch out. This man is a potential tyrant." When I see a woman nervously moving her wedding band back and forth on her wedding finger, I often assume she is suffering from the itch — or more probably she and her husband are not getting along too well.

No, you may not be able to directly control your feelings, but you can control your thoughts and actions voluntarily. Therefore, in the strength of Christ, master your thoughts and actions and thus dominate your feelings.

It is impossible for you to "rejoice in the Lord always" and to worry at the same time. Furthermore, you cannot remove worry thoughts and fear thoughts by simply saying, "I don't want to be afraid. I don't want to worry."

If you would win over worry, discipline yourself to think upon the "these things" of verse eight. Chapter 10 will give added insight on this subject. Let your actions accommodate themselves to your thoughts. Discipline yourself to smile, to maintain good posture, to talk with a musical voice in a dynamic manner — in short, to act in a manner compatible with these positive thoughts.

Don't start tomorrow; start *today*. Start *now*. Your worries will flee. God will be glorified.

Much damage is done to the cause of Christ by professing Christians who shout out their defeatism and negativism by the limp manner with which they shake hands, the listless way in which they walk, the sourpuss countenance they maintain, and the plaintive and whining way in which they speak. I believe that these people do more damage to the cause of Christ than all of the bootleggers, extortionists, whoremongers, drunkards and the riffraff of society's gutter put together.

Several years ago as pastor of a large church in a Southern city I faced problems that would have challenged my sanity had it not been for the grace of God. Though it was kept from the congregation. several of the leaders and I learned that one of the senior deacons was enmeshed in sin. To make matters worse, he showed no signs of remorse and evidenced no desire to repent. Evidence was also uncovered indicating that another prominent member was stealing over $100.00 a week from the Sunday school offerings. The pressure was on. The question was, "What shall we do? Shall it be made public? If it is made public, will not the testimony of Christ suffer irreparably? Will not the witness for God be hampered irremediably for years to come?"

In addition to these problems my wife and I had a sorrow in our home. Our precious little son was totally paralyzed. He suffered from cerebral palsy as the result of birth injuries caused by an intoxicated doctor who has since committed suicide. The little fellow was hovering between life and death. Where was the answer to my despondency?

My mind was drawn to Psalm 1. As never before I learned to appreciate the wisdom of that blessed man who delights in the law of the Lord *day and night.* I did not want to feel as I was feeling. It was not a good testimony. Therefore, by God's grace I fastened my thoughts upon the "these things" of Philippians 4:8 and endeavored to act in a compatible manner. On several occasions I would get into my car, drive outside the city, and literally force myself to laugh and to sing. I'm sure some passersby thought I was crazy. This procedure kept me from going crazy!

Think and act the way God would have you to think and act. Result? You will feel as you think and act. This will glorify God. It will help you give worry the brush-off.

6

Count Your Many Blessings

If you would utilize this tonic of praise as an antidote to worry, you must *count your many blessings*.

Here again you must "gird up the loins of your mind" and with sheer determined effort force yourself, if necessary, to focus your attention upon all of the blessings God has so lavishly bestowed upon you. Read the Psalms for help in this.

Your blessings may not be material blessings. But they are real blessings, nevertheless. Actually, no man has ever found joy simply because he acquired material gain. Joy does not consist in the abundance of our material possessions.

> . . . for a man's life consisteth not in the abundance of the things which he possesseth. (Luke 12:15b)

For how much money would you sell the health that God has given to you? How much does your wife's love mean to you? Have you ever thoroughly evaluated the value of your child's devotion? For what amount would you sell your reputation if it could be put on the open market? What premium do you put upon the eyesight God has given you — and the capacity to hear, and to speak, and to feel, and to taste? Have you ever thought how impoverished you would be if suddenly you were to be deprived of all your friends?

We tend to take the manifold blessings of God for granted, don't we? Start counting your blessings; your heart will overflow with gratitude and your lips with praise.

You know the old story about the king who was so unhappy he dispatched one of his men to go on a trip and find a happy man. The king ordered, "When you find the happy man, purchase his shirt and bring it back to me that I might wear it and also be happy." For years the king's man traveled and searched. He could not find a happy man. Finally, one day when he was walking in one of the poorer sections of one of the most impoverished countries he heard a man singing at the top of his voice. He followed the sound and found a man who was plowing a field. He asked the plowman, "Are you happy?"

The plowman replied, "I have never known a day of unhappiness."

The king's representative then told the plowman the purpose of his mission.

The plowman laughed uproariously as he replied, "Why, man, I don't have a shirt!"

"I had the blues because I had no shoes
Until upon the street I met a man who had no feet."

Count your blessings. If it will help you, periodically take a piece of paper and write out your blessings. Praise God for the love of your wife, the affection of your children, your good health, the encouragement of your friends. As you exert some effort along this line, blessings by the score will come crowding into your consciousness and you will jump to your feet, your heart singing, "Praise God from whom all blessings flow!" And you will be honoring the Lord in obeying the exhortation of verse four.

> How precious also are thy thoughts unto me, O God! how great is the sum of them!
> If I should count them, they are more in number than the sand: when I awake, I am still with thee.
>
> (Psalm 139:17,18)

> Many, O Lord my God, are thy wonderful works which thou hast done, and thy thoughts which are to us-ward: they cannot be reckoned up in order unto thee: if I would declare and speak of them, they are more than can be numbered.
>
> (Psalm 40:5)

Spurgeon, the great Baptist preacher of the last century, wrote of a young man who had suffered an accident in which he had broken his hip. The hip did not heal properly and it left the man crippled. Earnestly the people prayed that God would restore this young man to health and strength. Shortly after the people began their intense and concerted intercession on behalf of this young man, apparent tragedy struck. Yes, the young man fell and broke his hip again. Was it tragedy? It would have been completely natural for him and for the intercessors to begin to complain, for it seemed as though the condition was much worse. Fortunately many of the intercessors — wise and mature Christians — saw God's hand in the entire affair. They began praising Him and thanking Him for the blessing. Now the hip was set properly. It wasn't long until convalescence under God's leadership had done its perfect work. The young man walked with no limp whatsoever. The tragedy was a blessing.

Count your blessings! Even when things seem to go wrong, thank God and take courage. Say with the Apostle Paul,

> Most gladly, therefore, will I rather glory in my infirmities that the power of Christ may rest upon me.
>
> (2 Corinthians 12:9b)

In 1950 the Lord blessed us with a precious baby boy. Due to a tragedy described in detail a little later in this book the little fellow nearly died. God was pleased to spare him, but he was now totally paralyzed. He had a keen mind and normal inclinations and desires, but his body would not respond to the demands of his will. Oh, yes, it hurt — hurt him and hurt us. However, God gave him a marvelously sweet disposition.

Was his paralysis and condition as a cerebral palsy victim a blessing? Yes. *Definitely so.* Between the year of his birth and the year I resigned the pastorate to go into full-time evangelism I undoubtedly buried more little babies and small children and ministered to more sick children than any man in any pastorate. God had conditioned me in a special way for a peculiar and yet a blessed ministry that He was about to entrust to me. The life of my son was a distinct blessing. There are many ways in which I could demonstrate this, but they involve experiences locked up in the cherished and secret places of my heart and open only to God and our immediate family.

"Count your blessings. Name them one by one, and it will surprise you what the Lord has done." And one of the greatest surprises will be the fact that you are no longer saddled by that monster, worry, who has been riding herd on you.

Let me urge again that when you become depressed and worried, take a piece of paper and literally force yourself to write out in detail every blessing that comes to mind. Concentrate. Think hard. Surely it will take time, but not as much time as worrying will. It won't take as much time as an interview at the psychiatrist's office and it will be considerably cheaper. Furthermore, in the strength of God you will be actively doing something about your own condition. This is much more effective than passively responding to psychotherapy.*

In Chapter 7 consideration is given to a most important factor in the matter of praise.

---

*Please do not misconstrue what has been written as an expression of disregard for the effectiveness of psychiatry and for its essential importance in certain situations. Nevertheless, there are many people who today are frequenting the offices of psychiatrists who could be enjoying mental and emotional health had they only taken certain precautions and observed the biblical formula — Praise Plus Poise Plus Prayer Equal Peace — earlier in their life.

7

Anticipate Apathy

In other words, don't expect to be appreciated. When you are appreciated it will be like the cherry on top of the whipped cream of your strawberry sundae — something a little special.

Let not your rejoicing be dependent upon appreciation shown to you.

Our Lord healed ten lepers. Do you remember how many came back to thank Him? That's right. One!

The late General Harry C. Trexler, a wealthy philanthropist and outstanding citizen of Allentown, Pennsylvania, was providing the financial needs for forty college students in 1933, the year in which he died. Four months before his death he called his secretary in and inquired how many young men and women he was sending through college. She told him. With mixed bewilderment and grief he replied, "And last Christmas I got only one or two Christmas cards from this group."

Many times, when discussing this prevalent ingratitude, I have stated in a jocular vein, "Would you believe it? Why there are some people who don't even appreciate me!"

Expect ingratitude. Give for the joy of giving and soon you

will be so thrillingly occupied with this privilege of giving, you will not have time to reflect upon the ingratitude of others.

Sometime ago I read about a man in New York who, over a period of more than four decades, helped more than 5,000 young people secure positions in New York City. When discussing it sometime later he observed that only six had expressed gratitude.

Years ago there was a shipwreck in Lake Michigan. A powerful swimmer who was then a student at Northwestern University rescued twenty-three persons before he finally collapsed. Some years after that, in Los Angeles, Dr. R. A. Torrey was telling the story about this young man's concern and his heroic deeds. To his astonishment he found out that the man, now old, was in the audience. In talking with the rescuer, he asked him what was the most significant thing about the rescue — the thing that stood out most in his memory after all the intervening years. The rescuer dropped his eyes and in a low voice said, "Not a one said 'thanks.'"

Have you ever read about Aristotle's ideal man? Here is the philosopher's definition of the ideal man. "The ideal man takes joy in doing favors for others; but he feels ashamed to have others do favors for him. For it is a mark of superiority to confer a kindness; but it is a mark of inferiority to receive it."

Paul reminded the Christians to whom he was speaking that "It is more blessed to give than to receive" (Acts 20:35). Therefore, let your joy arise out of the blessedness of giving, of helping, of doing. Not expecting gratitude, find your joy in the very act of service.

Years ago Samuel Johnson said, "Gratitude is a fruit of great cultivation. You do not find it among gross people."

It is quite evident as you read the Pauline Epistles that some of the very people whom Paul won to faith in Jesus Christ turned upon him and reviled him maliciously.

Do you know what is the basic sin? Someone answers, "Unbelief." No, if you will read Romans 1:21 you will conclude that ingratitude is at the root of all sin whether that ingratitude be active or whether it be passive.

> Because that, when they knew God, they glorified him not as God, neither were thankful; but became vain in their imaginations, and their foolish heart was darkened.
>
> (Romans 1:21)

Was not ingratitude the root of the sin committed by Adam and Eve?

Consider it. The Lord Jesus Christ died for us, "while we were yet sinners" (Romans 5:8). He suffered. He bled. He died — for *us*. Yet there are millions who, knowing this, refuse to accept Him as Savior and Lord. Why? Ingratitude!

Ingratitude is a universal sin. Expect it. Give for the joy of giving. Do for the joy of doing. Help only for the joy of helping. And you won't have time even to notice the prevalence of this sin, ingratitude.

Praise should be the habit pattern of your life regardless of the cold and even cruel treatment received from some whom you have helped.

8

Master the Art
of Altruism

If you would conquer worry with this weapon of *praise* you must master the art of altruism.

Become genuinely interested in other people. Love your neighbor as yourself. Honor God by losing your life in serving others. By "others" I am referring not only to your employer or your family, but also to all those whom God gives you the privilege of serving.

An upset, young college man sought counseling from Dr. George W. Truett who was pastor of First Baptist Church of Dallas, Texas at that time. The student had passed through troubled waters. He said he was ready to give up his faith and that he had lost all confidence in God and people. Wisely and patiently Dr. Truett listened to this young man. When the student finished his tale of woe, the wise and patient pastor asked the young man for a favor. The young man agreed. Dr. Truett then gave the young man the name of the hospital and the room number of a patient who was in need of a visit. Said the great-hearted minister, "I just don't have time to make the visit. You make it for me." The young man assented.

He came away from that hospital bed a new man. As a favor to the mighty pastor of Dallas, the young man determined to do his best. He did so well that he became genuinely interested in the patient. In so doing, his own difficulties and despair were dispelled.

Uncle Joe Hawk was one of the most radiant personalities I ever met. For more than half a century he was a member of the First Baptist Church of Cleveland, Tennessee. When I met him, he was eighty-seven years old but younger than many twenty-five-year-old people. He attended every service I conducted in that good church in 1953.

Let me tell you a little about him and you will catch an insight into his sparkling vitality at eighty-seven. Years before during the depression, the First Baptist Church of Cleveland, Tennessee was in straitened circumstances. Uncle Joe Hawk was a drayman. He had been blessed with a good business, but of course he was suffering as were the other businessmen during those oppressive years. Nevertheless, he forgot himself. This dear man lost himself in his concern for that church and its people, many of whom had not yet accepted Christ.

At the risk of putting a calamitous crimp in his business, Uncle Joe sold his two finest dray horses. He gave the money to the church. Because of his gift the First Baptist Church of Cleveland, Tennessee, stands as a mighty citadel for Christ today. Few people knew what he did. He did it without fanfare. In fact, many of the church members today are unaware of this tremendous sacrifice. Uncle Joe never got the money back from the church. He didn't expect to. He didn't want it. He gave it for the sheer joy of giving. He gave it to the eternal glory of God and for the spiritual profit of man. No man who is that interested in others has time to worry about his own problems.

When was the last time you sacrificed and sent anonymously a gift of $50.00 over and above your tithe to a college or seminary student who was having a hard time? When was the last time you gave something to someone anonymously — something that could in no wise profit you from a material standpoint?

Perhaps the mother next door is sick and in great need of help. Why not offer to take care of the children for a couple of days? True, they may be little monsters. That is all the more reason your help would be a great benefit to their mother. When your neighbor goes on vacation, why not offer to take care of the mail and send it on? Why not drop a line of appreciation to that teacher who has taken such an interest in your child and has made such a distinct contribution to his highest good? Drop a line of gratitude to your pastor for the message that was such a blessing to you. Encourage him. It will take only a few moments of time and a stamp.

Does not the Word of God tell us we are to esteem others better than ourselves?

> Let nothing be done through strife or vainglory; but in lowliness of mind let each esteem other better than themselves.   (Philippians 2:3)

Let me earnestly suggest that you determine to do something specific for someone everyday — something for which no remuneration of any kind will be sought or expected. You may exclaim, "Shades of the Boy Scouts!" but this is good religion and besides, it will relieve you of that time you normally give to worrying. Your cup will run over with the joy of the Lord.

Go ahead, do it *now*. If it doesn't come to you easily and if you don't know how to begin, simply sit down and ask the Lord to guide you. With pencil and paper write down some things that come to your mind.

Perhaps the Lord will lead you to do the washing for the lady next door who has been hampered by her day-and-night care of sick children. Perhaps you will contact the head of some fine Christian college or one of our seminaries to secure the name of a student who is in great need. You will help him. You may be led to invite a serviceman to have dinner with you on Sunday (we are not as thoughtful along that line as we were during the war years). There is no point in my going on; you take it from here.

By all means, use common sense in your efforts to assist other people. Don't be like a certain young cub scout who had his own ideas on the subject. One night during a pack meeting the scoutmaster asked all those who had done their good deed for the day to lift their hands. All hands were lifted except the hand of one scout.

The scoutmaster barked out, "Johnny, go out and do your good deed for the day and don't come back until you have done it."

Johnny left. He was gone about twenty minutes. He came back. His clothes were in shreds. His hair was disheveled. His face was cut and bleeding.

The scoutmaster said, "Johnny, what have you been doing?"

Johnny replied, "I did my good deed for the day, sir."

"What was that?" asked the scoutmaster.

"I helped an old lady across the street, sir."

"Well," said the scoutmaster, "how did you get in that condition?"

"She didn't want to go," replied Johnny.

Use common sense in your effort to help others. During the darkest part of the depression a needy family was given an expensive pedigreed French poodle. Doubtless there is much good to be said about a French poodle. But the friend who gave the dog would have been much wiser and more helpful if she had taken the same money and purchased needed clothing and food for the family.

Assist the other person at the point of his greatest need. While doing so, remember "It is more blessed to give than to receive" (Acts 20:35).

Your genuine interest in other people will assassinate the monster of worry. Your positive thoughts of concern for others will crowd out the negative fear-producing thoughts of worry.

Reflect once again upon the concern our Lord showed for others. Even while dying, He cried out, "Father, forgive them for they know not what they do." While in the agonizing process of dying upon the cross He showed concern for His mother and made the finest possible preparation for her after His departure.

Man is as selfish as he dares to be. We are selfish by nature. The middle letter of sin is "I." The middle letter of pride is "I." It takes the cross experience to adequately cancel out the "I." Real Christian discipline in the strength of God is required to master the art of altruism, but the rewards are immeasurable — especially as they relate to the altruist.

Without exception the people who are always rejoicing are people who have mastered this art of altruism — people who are genuinely interested in others. This rejoicing chases gloom and kills worry.

You will "rejoice in the Lord always" as you faithfully fulfill the injunction in Galatians 6:2-4:

> Bear ye one another's burdens, and so fulfil the law of Christ. For if a man think himself to be something, when he is nothing, he deceiveth himself. But let every man prove his own work, and then shall he have *rejoicing* in himself alone, and not in another.

I share with you these same verses in the *Amplified New Testament:*

> Bear (endure, carry) one another's burdens and trouble-some moral thoughts, and in this way fulfill and observe perfectly the law of Christ, the Messiah, and complete what is lacking (in your obedience to it). For if any person thinks himself to be somebody (too important to condescend to shoulder another's load), when he is nobody (of superiority except in his own estimation), he deceives and deludes and cheats himself. But let every person carefully scrutinize and examine and test his own conduct and his own work. He can then have the personal satisfaction and joy of doing something commendable (in itself alone) without (resorting to) boastful comparison with his neighbor.   (Galatians 6:2-4)

Part 3

Poise

9

Our Impelling
Motive

> Let your moderations be known unto all men. The Lord is
> at hand.   (Philippians 4:5)

> Have a reputation for gentleness, and never forget the
> nearness of your Lord.   (Philippians 4:5 — Phillips)

Now listen to the fuller translation of the *Amplified New
Testament:*

> Let all men know and perceive and recognize your un-
> selfishness — your considerateness, your forbearing spirit.
> The Lord is near — He is coming soon.

The word translated in the King James "moderation" can
also be translated "suitable," "fair," "reasonable," "gen-
tle," "mild," "patient," and "lenient." The word further
carries the idea of "congeniality of spirit." After making a
thorough study of the word you will inevitably conclude that I
have spelled it correctly — poise — for according to Webster
the word *poise* means "balance," "stability," "ease,"
"dignity of manner," etc.

What is the supreme inducement to poise? What is our
impelling motive? What is the driving force that pushes us
toward this goal? Here it is in a brief and meaningful message! "The Lord is near." This is a literal translation of the

words in the King James, "the Lord is at hand." In fact, the actual translation would be, "the Lord near." Three words! No verb was used. It was not needed. It is abrupt to the point of the dramatic. It is a bolt of light.

The awareness of His nearness gives great calm in the storm and stress of life.

Fortune may have eluded you. Culture which you have sought so laboriously becomes ever more painfully remote. Professed love has betrayed you. All these may be true. But "the Lord is near"! There is no mockery in that statement. Those few words assure us, and they impel us to observe the mandates set down in Philippians 4:4-8.

This truth gives urgency and charm to the admonition set down by Paul in this fourth chapter of Philippians.

This statement can refer to Christ's nearness to us right now or to His Second Coming. The best interpreters so agree.

John Calvin, Bishop Moule, and Dean Vaughan all prefer the thought of Christ's present nearness. On the other hand, equally great teachers and commentators such as Dean Alford, F. B. Meyer, and Bishop Lightfoot, prefer the interpretation which is eschatological. They believe the emphasis is on the Second Coming of Christ.

Let us take advantage of the insights of both groups of commentators.

The Lord is near *locally.* "Thou art near, O Lord," sang the psalmist (Psalm 119:151a). And the Apostle Paul echoes and glorifies the ancient song.

The Lord is near in that He indwells, by the Holy Spirit, the individual Christian. It is "Christ in you" (Colossians 1:27).

Then the Lord is near from the standpoint of His *availability.* The psalmist cried, "The Lord is nigh unto all them that call upon him" (Psalm 145:18). Here again the New Testament echoes the Old Testament. As children of God we have His ear because we have His heart. A distant Lord would depress us and distress us. An unapproachable Savior could not help us. Thank God, Christ is approachable.

> For we have not an high priest which cannot be touched with the feeling of our infirmities; but was in all points tempted like as we are, yet without sin.
>
> Let us therefore come boldly unto the throne of grace, that we may obtain mercy, and find grace to help in time of need.
>
> (Hebrews 4:15,16)

In the exigencies and vicissitudes of life the Lord is near. The psalmist anticipated this truth again. He sang, ''The Lord is nigh unto all them that are of a broken heart'' (Psalm 34:18). Who has not known the distressful mystery of a broken heart! ''God is . . . a very present help in trouble'' (Psalm 46:1). The consciousness of Christ's availability induces poise.

Then the Lord is at hand *eschatologically*. He is coming again in clouds of heaven with great glory. I believe His coming is sooner than we think. Very real to the early Christians was the return of our Lord. He Himself declared it in no ambiguous terms.

Jesus may come today. In the silence and darkness of midnight His trumpet may sound and His awful glory blaze upon us!

Our love of His appearing is the greatest inducement to obedience of this admonition to poise in Philippians 4:5. Every injunction mentioned in this book — injunctions all rooted in His divine mandate to us — is more easily fulfilled when we are motivated by the continuous consciousness of the possibility that Jesus may come today. ''Be ye also ready'' (Matthew 24:44).

The return of our Lord viewed as possibly near should make us rich in Christian character. Contemplation of this truth will make us like Him who is our great Exemplar.

Remember the King James translation of verse 5, ''Let your moderation be known unto all men. The Lord is at hand.'' The preferable translation of the last sentence is, ''The Lord is near.'' The greatest inducement to poise is the consciousness of the nearness of your Lord. This is the greatest impelling motive to that poise that combats worry.

As you live in the consciousness of the nearness of the Lord, you will find strength that will enable you to observe the biblical formula for peace. You will find strength and inclination to observe the factors involved in the matter of praise.

You will find the factors relating to poise much easier to fulfill as you live in the consciousness of the nearness of your Lord. For instance, you will find that your thoughts are thoughts that please Him and therefore positive thoughts that will put worry on the run. As you live in the consciousness of His nearness you will realize a strength, not your own, enabling you to exercise the self-control that leads to poise and banishes worry.

You will also have victory in the matter of relaxation as you live in the consciousness of the nearness of your Lord.

In the matter of scheduling, the consciousness of the Lord's nearness is a great boon. We avail ourselves of His help. We know that "The steps of a good man are ordered by the Lord" (Psalm 37:23).

Living in the consciousness of the nearness of our Lord will dispel the clouds of pessimism and lead us into the sunshine of enthusiasm and optimism. You cannot live in the consciousness of His nearness and go around looking as if you were born in crab apple time, put up in vinegar and weaned on a dill pickle. People who act as though they were born in the kickative mood and the objective case are those who live oblivious to the nearness of the Lord.

With respect to every factor mentioned in Part 3 of this book, fulfillment is largely contingent upon your awareness of the nearness of the Lord.

It goes without saying that Part 4 — "Prayer" — of this book is meaningless apart from the consciousness of the nearness of the Lord.

To sum up: The Lord is near *locally*. That should remind us that He is watching everything we do. The Lord is at hand with respect to His *availability*. That assures us of the needed resources to fulfill our every responsibility to Him and for

Him. The Lord is at hand *eschatologically*. That reminds us He may come at any time. This induces us always to live in a way that would not shame us if He were to burst unexpectedly upon the scene.

In these three words, then — *the Lord near* — lies dynamic truth. These words are the steam of motive power generating attitudes and activities in fulfillment of the divine demands.

10

Poise Through Thought Control

> Finally, brethren, whatsoever things are true, whatsoever things are honest, whatsoever things are just, whatsoever things are pure, whatsoever things are lovely, whatsoever things are of good report; if there be any virtue, and if there be any praise, think on these things.   (Philippians 4:8)

> For as he thinketh in his heart, so is he: Eat and drink, saith he to thee; but his heart is not with thee.   (Proverbs 23:7)

In Chapter 5 the truth was set forth that while we cannot control our feelings directly, we can control them indirectly by controlling our thoughts.

You can control your thoughts directly if you so desire. To be sure, it will take some discipline. Arnold Bennett, in his splendid book, *How to Live on Twenty-Four Hours a Day*, challenges the reader to think on any given subject every day for at least fifteen minutes without permitting his mind to wander. I challenge you to try it.

Many people can brood for fifteen minutes. They can worry for fifteen minutes. But very few people can focus their attention on any given, and I might add worthwhile, subject for fifteen minutes without permitting their minds to wander.

To repeat a statement previously made in this book, you

cannot think fear and act courage. If you want victory over anxiety, you must develop the control of your thoughts which leads to that poise that conquers worry.

The wisest man of history assures us that we are what we think. That is true. In the words of Marcus Aurelius, "A man's life is what his thoughts make of it." Ralph Waldo Emerson states the truth in another way when he says, "A man is what he thinks about all day long." Our dominant thoughts tend to externalize themselves.

It's an old trick, but school children still love to play it. One will go to Billy and say, "Say, you look terrible. Are you feeling well today?" A little later another one will approach him with a similar suggestion. And then a third. And a fourth. Soon the thought of his not being well becomes Billy's dominant thought — and he goes home sick!

In my first pastorate there was a young lady twenty-nine years of age who maintained an expression on her face that looked like the advance agent of a coming cyclone. She *enjoyed* poor health! Her house was a mess and her general appearance looked like an accident going somewhere to happen. She would come out the front door after the church service and I would shake her hand. It was so limp I felt like handing it back to her. I would say, "How are you?" She would then proceed to tell her tale of woe. I was only twenty-two years old, but I learned one lesson in a hurry. I stopped asking her how she was. When I shook her hand, I *shook* it, believe me! I gave her my finest smile and said, calling her by name, "You look so much better. You must be feeling better." Believe it or not, within a few months she was looking better and apparently feeling better. With the help of some friends I dropped a seed thought into her mind which became a dominant thought and as she thought, so she became.

Paul says to think on the things that are true. Don't think on falsehood. Think on falsehood and pretty soon you will become false. Your heart will condemn you and your worries will increase.

Think on things that are honest, not dishonest. Your

thoughts will tend to externalize themselves. If you think honestly, you live honestly. The word here could be translated, "honorable." Think on things that are honorable. Even if it is true, refuse to think about it if it's dishonorable.

Think on things that are pure. The word used here refers to all sorts of purity. As Peter would say, "Gird up the loins of your mind" (1 Peter 1:13a). An impure thought always precedes an impure deed. Keep your thoughts pure and your deeds will be pure. Pure thoughts are incompatible with worry thoughts.

Think on things that are lovely. This word means "winsome and pleasing." As you embrace thoughts that are winsome and pleasing you will bar from entrance thoughts that produce worry and anxiety.

The Apostle Paul says, "Think on things of good report." The words *good report* come from two words meaning "fair-speaking." It could also be translated "attractive." Attractive thoughts will also deliver you from worry. Attractive thoughts will deliver you from being a sourpuss.

Paul then said, "If there be any virtue, and if there be any praise, think on these things." The word *virtue* comes from a word *aresko* which means "to please." Here again learn to control your thoughts so they will relate to that which pleases; they will be pleasing thoughts.

Under God, control your thoughts. Some people are miserable because they are indiscriminate with respect to the guests they invite into their minds. They think worry thoughts, fear thoughts, anxiety thoughts. They don't see the glass half full, they always see it half empty. They are not optimistic, they are pessimistic. They pride themselves by sanctimoniously saying, "I expect the worst so that I will never be disappointed." Expect the worst and you will get the worst. Thoughts of the worst when dominating your life tend to externalize themselves into your outward actions so that you become the creator of the worst. You therefore create a self-destroying monster.

Do your own thinking. You must guard yourself even against the well-meaning but oftentimes negative influences and damaging advice of relatives and friends. They mean well, but they often do much damage. Don't leave your mind open to the negative influence of other people. Read the biography of any dynamic personality — any achiever — and almost without exception you will discover that discouraging remarks, poor advice, negative influences, and downright opposition were thrown across his path by the people who were the closest to him.

Misery loves company and worriers will do their best to drag you down to their level.

There were two farmers. One was a pessimist, the other was an optimist.

The optimist would say, "Wonderful sunshine."

The pessimist would respond, "Yeah, I'm afraid it's going to scorch the crops."

The optimist would say, "Fine rain."

The pessimist would respond, "Yeah, I'm afraid we are going to have a flood."

One day the optimist said to the pessimist, "Have you seen my new bird dog? He's the finest money can buy."

The pessimist said, "You mean that mutt I saw penned up behind your house? He don't look like much to me."

The optimist said, "How about going hunting with me tomorrow?" The pessimist agreed. They went. They shot some ducks. The ducks landed on the pond. The optimist ordered his dog to get the ducks. The dog obediently responded. Instead of swimming in the water after the ducks, the dog walked on top of the water, retrieved the ducks, and walked back on top of the water.

The optimist turned to the pessimist and said, "Now, what do you think of that?"

Whereupon the pessimist replied, "Hmm, he can't swim, can he?"

In the strength of God, control your thoughts. Let them be regulated according to the will of God. Such thoughts will lead to inner poise that is a shield against worry.

11

Poise Through Self-Control

Study the records of those whom the world calls great and you will observe that every one of them possesses this quality of self-control.

Many homes are wrecked through lack of self-control. Only God knows the number of churches whose testimonies have been irreparably neutralized simply because of this prevalent lack of self-control among the leadership. Businessmen by the thousands who are capable and qualified in every other respect receive only a fraction of their income potential due to this lack of self-control.

Never retaliate against your enemies. In so doing you may force them to pay the price of grief, but the resultant price of your own grief will be greater. The Bible tells us that we must love our enemies (Matthew 5:44).

While you are hating your enemies you are giving them the sovereignty of your own life. You are literally forcing them to dominate you. For instance, here is a man who has wronged you. You loathe him. Your loathing becomes a festering personality-sore. You so detest him you would not welcome him into your home. You would not permit him to fraternize with your relatives. You would not invite him to eat at your table or spend the night in your guest room. Yet, all the time, while you are hating him you are "entertaining" him in your blood stream, in your brain cells, in your nerve fibers, in your muscles, and in the marrow of your bones. You are giving him power over your sleep, power over your blood pressure, power over your health, power over your happiness. You are *insisting* that he destroy your body and disintegrate your effectiveness. *Tragic!*

Some years ago *Life* carried an article on high blood pressure. In that article the statement was made that the chief personality trait of people with high blood pressure is resentment. What a price to pay for lack of self-control! They are paying financially in doctors' bills and medical assistance. They are paying emotionally with shattered nerves. They are paying in reduced efficiency resulting in decreased income. They are paying domestically in strife in the home resulting from the projection of their bitterness and misery. *What a price!*

Learn a lesson from our Lord in whose steps we are commanded to follow:

> Who, when he was reviled, reviled not again; when he suffered, he threatened not; but committed himself to him that judgeth righteously. (1 Peter 2:23)

Well did the wise Solomon say:

> Better . . . is he that ruleth his spirit than he that taketh a city. (Proverbs 16:32b)

Reflect for a moment upon the poise of the immortal Lincoln. In the anguish of his most grief-producing hours, he exercised poise. Had it not been for this quality it is doubtful that the war between the states would have ended in victory for the Union Army. It is highly doubtful his name would have been immortalized had it not been for this magnificent quality. Men in his own cabinet were disloyal to him, trying on several occasions to discredit him. To his back they made light of him, scoffed at his limited education, and sneered at his rustic ways. Realizing that their disloyalty was to him personally, and realizing further that they possessed qualities making them essential to our nation, the ex-rail-splitter exercised self-control, disregarding the objectional characteristics of these colleagues.

In attaining the mastery of self-control you must learn how to *conquer criticism*. I do not mean that you can avoid criticism. Nor do I mean that you can subdue criticism. You can conquer it, however, with respect to its relationship *to you* personally.

Once again follow the example of our Lord who answered His critics so often with silence. Our Lord defended other people. He defended the Word of God. He defended the work of His Heavenly Father. He defended little children. *He never defended Himself!*

Usually you will find it wise not to answer your critics.

> Answer not a fool according to his folly, lest thou also be like unto him.   (Proverbs 26:4)

Your friends don't need an answer and your enemies won't believe the answer.

Unjust criticism is often a disguised compliment. It often indicates that you have excited the jealousy and envy of the critic. As the old adage goes, "No one ever kicks a dead dog."

It is wise to listen to criticism of yourself, but do it objectively. While listening, don't allow yourself to become emotionally involved. Sometimes you can profit greatly. If the criticism is just, do something about it. If the criticism is unjust, put it where you put your other garbage.

Clergymen are often criticized! If the minister wears a black suit, the critics say, "Who does he think he is — Digger O'Dell?" If he wears a sport coat, the critics question, "What is he trying to do, imitate a movie star?" If he has five children they respond, "He can't afford such a family. Why doesn't he use better sense?" If he has only one child they quip, "Doesn't he know the Bible says that we are to be 'fruitful and multiply'?" If he visits the poor they say he is showing off. If he visits the rich they say he is playing politics. If he drives a Buick they say he ought to drive a car priced within his means. If he drives a Volkswagon, they say, "What's he trying to do, embarrass us by letting people think we don't pay him enough?" If he preaches thirty minutes, they say he is long-winded. If he preaches twenty minutes they say, "What's the matter, didn't he study last week?" If he goes away to conduct meetings in another church they complain, "He ought to stay home and take care of the flock." If he stays home and never goes away, they howl, "What's the matter, doesn't anyone else want him either?" My father gave me some good advice when I entered the ministry. He said, "John, listen to what people say when they are mad. That's what they really mean."

A man flies off the handle. He says some nasty things. After he cools down he comes back and says, "I really didn't mean that." Of course he meant it! If he had not thought it, he would not have said it, for God's Word makes it clear that, "Out of the abundance of the heart the mouth speaketh" (Matthew 12:34b). He didn't draw those words and thoughts out of thin air. They were in his heart.

While I am no disciple of Freud, I do believe in the so-called Freudian slips. When a person writes me a letter in longhand and he crosses out one word and writes down another, I may spend fifteen or twenty minutes holding that letter up to the light trying to decipher the word crossed out. In all probability that was what he really meant.

When you respond to criticism volcanically, you lose possession of many of your faculties so that your thoughts become inaccurate, your decisions unwise, and your words regrettable.

Let me tell you a little habit I have formed which has served me well. By nature I am very explosive. After all, I am half Syrian and people from that part of the world are not usually phlegmatic. When God called me into the ministry, He impressed upon me the fact that by His grace my spirit must be completely dominated by Him if I were to be an effective ambassador of the Court of Heaven. I memorized and meditated upon 2 Timothy 2:24 and 25.

> And the servant of the Lord must not strive; but be gentle
> unto all men, apt to teach, patient. In meekness instructing
> those that oppose themselves; if God peradventure will give
> them repentance to the acknowledging of the truth.

Now here is the procedure I have followed when the
provocation of unjust criticism has sorely tempted me to lose
my head. Through sheer conscious effort I listen objectively.
I look at the person who is venting his anger, but I do not see
him, for in my mind's eye I am watching a moving picture. A
huge elephant is walking down the street. I picture myself as
that elephant. Over by the curb (and I am inclined sometimes
to think, in the gutter) there's a little ant who is spitting at the
elephant. Rather ludicrous, you say. Precisely. It helps my
sense of humor. Now then, does the elephant stop and
threaten the ant? Of course not. The elephant is unaware of
the puny efforts of this pompous ant.

All I can say is that this certainly works for me and I have
no copyright on it. It keeps me in complete possession of my
faculties so that I can think clearly and quickly, talk judi-
ciously, and act wisely.

An American statesman was once quoted as saying,
"Never lose your temper except when you do it on purpose."
That's a good statement and one that will bear much thought.

Let's go back to Abraham Lincoln for just a moment.
While he was an occupant of the White House, some
loquacious "smut-sprayers" and "character assassinators"
spread the rumor that he was living with a black woman.
What did the President do? Nothing. This man of poise had
learned that in a fight with a skunk you might win the fight,
but you will smell awful!

If as you've been reading these last few paragraphs you
have caught yourself chuckling a time or two, good. Don't
take yourself too seriously.

A vital relationship with God through Christ will result in
self-control and you will refuse to respond to criticism with
smug complacence, worldly courtesy, patronizing conde-
scension, or vindictive retaliation. You will respond with
love which is not compatible with fear, the basis of worry.

There is no fear in love; but perfect love casteth out fear: because fear hath torment. He that feareth is not made perfect in love.   (1 John 4:18)

12

Poise Through Enthusiasm

Once again let me remind you that by poise we are referring to gentleness, fairness, congeniality of spirit.

Enthusiasm is an indispensable ingredient. Some pseudo-intellectuals may take exception to this. I reply simply that most of what we do is done on the basis of emotional impulse rather than intellectual impulse. I do not love my next door neighbor because of an intellectual theory regarding him. Rather I love him because of an emotional impulse. You did not buy that insurance policy because you intend to die tomorrow and because through intellectual activity you arrived at that sobering possibility. The main inducement was strictly emotional. You saw your family destitute and in want because of inadequate material resources. It was the emotional reaction of this that led you to buy the insurance policy. You go to a football game. There you can tell no difference in behavior between the man with a third-grade education and the man with several doctor's degrees. They both respond emotionally, with enthusiasm.

One of my hobbies is reading books on salesmanship. I have a collection of over forty. Without exception each book on salesmanship underscores enthusiasm as an essential quality for success.

The leaders of this world always have been and are men of enthusiasm. Adolph Hitler knew the power of enthusiasm. His formula for speaking was "Say it simply. Say it often. *Make it burn*." And the Austrian "paper hanger" became a world figure who could not be ignored. Paul the apostle was a man of enthusiasm as his own autobiographical remarks in Galatians 1:14 and Acts 22:3 attest. He was so enthusiastic about the Gospel he preached, that some of the people in Corinth accused him of madness (2 Corinthians 5:13).

The man who never wonders at anything never does anything wonderful. That partially explains why the work of the Lord suffers so across the land. Thousands of people who profess a relationship with God through Jesus Christ have apparently failed to grasp what Christ has done for us and what are our privileges in Him. Therefore they come to church on Sunday morning with a face long enough to eat ice cream out of a pipe. You could ruin the greatest football team in the nation if you would fill the grandstands for four consecutive games with the average Sunday morning congregation.

No wonder communism spreads while the religion of Jesus Christ fails to keep pace with the population increase of the world. One thing you must say for the Communists — they are enthusiastic about their cause. Next Sunday when you go to church, watch the average person as he comes in. He shuffles along dragging his lower lip behind him. Then he slides into the pew and hangs his lower lip over the pew in front of him. He looks as happy as the skeleton and crossbones on an iodine bottle. No wonder he has no peace of mind. Remember Chapter 5. You cannot act one way and feel another way. When you act sour, you are sour.

Some people who profess "religion" have talked about it for so long in negative terms and in pessimistic platitudes that a distorted concept has made its way into the thinking of the people whom they influence.

I heard of a man who walked into a hotel lobby and stood beside another man at the room clerk's counter. The fellow eyed his neighbor for a moment and then could not restrain himself from asking, "Are you a preacher?"

"No," said the neighbor, "I've just been sick!"

And I can well understand the little girl who came home from Sunday school and going up to Betsy, the mule, lovingly stroked her long head and said, "Bless you, Betsy, you must be a wonderful Christian. You look just like Grandma."

Not only is a lack of enthusiasm ruinous to the work of the Lord, it is also ruinous to happiness in the home, success in business, the making and keeping of friends, and achievement in any field.

There is no such thing as a well-adjusted personality apart from enthusiasm. There is no such thing as a satisfactory social relationship apart from enthusiasm. You reap what you sow. You sow the wind and you get the whirlwind. You sow a dead-pan expression and that is exactly what you reap from the people with whom you associate. For what you give you receive in kind, but in greater degree. That is a fact that cannot be gainsaid.

It was my privilege to have an interview with Ray Jenkins, the brilliant lawyer from Knoxville, Tennessee, who presided over the Army-McCarthy hearings. In the course of conversation I asked him his formula for success in speaking. He mentioned several things, but one thing remains paramount in my mind. "Don't ever speak on a subject about which you are not totally enthused." This statement came from the lips of a man who is considered by the people of Tennessee, and of the United States for that matter, to be one of America's outstanding trial lawyers.

> Whatsoever thy hand findeth to do, do it with thy might;
> for there is no work, nor device, nor knowledge, nor wisdom,
> in the grave, whither thou goest.   (Ecclesiastes 9:10)

Enthusiasm is essential to *industry* which is discussed in Chapter 18. Enthusiasm is like steam. It impels action. Many people never become enthusiastic over anything, therefore they never *do* anything. Their lives become idle and negative and worrisome.

Enthusiasm tones up the whole life. You know men, and so do I, who constantly complain that they don't get enough sleep. They lament that they wake up every morning feeling as tired as when they went to bed. But what happens when they plan a fishing trip? They are awake before the alarm sounds at four o'clock in the morning — and feeling great! The explanation? Enthusiasm! All things being equal, the person who is enthusiastic turns out three and four times as much work as the person who is listless.

No great work has ever been done without enthusiasm. I give to God all the glory for the ministry of Billy Sunday. But let me state it flatly. Had it not been for his enthusiasm it is highly doubtful he would have so influenced this nation and even the world through a ministry that could not be ignored. Brother, he was enthusiastic!

To be sure, some people seem to be born with a greater capacity for enthusiasm than others. However, this is a quality that can be developed. It is developed by focusing the mind upon a worthwhile goal until the attainment of that goal becomes your "Magnificent Obsession."

The salesmen who succeed are enthusiastic salesmen. Musicians who succeed are enthusiastic musicians. Watch Leonard Bernstein on television! Have you not heard of some musicians who became so engrossed in their practice that they forgot even to take their meals? Ponder the enthusiasm of scientists at Cape Canaveral and Huntsville and other places who recently have been working day and night in perfecting our missile program and advancing the age of rocketry. I submit to you that their achievements would be impossible without enthusiasm.

Enthusiasm leads to achievement. A sense of achievement — an awareness of accomplishment — is indispensable to poise and to peace.

If you go about your daily responsibilities in a listless and lackadaisical spirit devoid of enthusiasm, you are doomed to failure. Your failure will create anxiety and worry. Anxiety and worry will create failure. Thus you become the duped victim of a vicious cycle.

Remember that you cannot focus your attention upon two thoughts at the same time. When you are enthused, you are focusing your attention upon thoughts that crowd out the thoughts producing fears and worry.

See what Paul suffered:

> Of the Jews five times received I forty stripes save one.
> Thrice was I beaten with rods, once was I stoned, thrice I suffered shipwreck, a night and a day I have been in the deep;
> In journeyings often, in perils of waters, in perils of robbers, in perils by mine own countrymen, in perils by the heathen, in perils in the city, in perils in the wilderness, in perils in the sea, in perils among false brethren;
> In weariness and painfulness, in watchings often, in hunger and thirst, in fastings often, in cold and nakedness.
> Beside those things that are without, that which cometh upon me daily, the care of all the churches.
>
> (2 Corinthians 11:24-28)

Did he worry? Did he fret? No! A godly enthusiasm delivered him from self-pity and worry. Ponder his poise — poise through enthusiasm.

> We are troubled on every side, yet not distressed; we are perplexed, but not in despair;
> Persecuted, but not forsaken; cast down, but not destroyed;
> For which cause we faint not; but though our outward man perish, yet the inward man is renewed day by day.
> For our light affliction, which is but for a moment, worketh for us a far more exceeding and eternal weight of glory.
>
> (2 Corinthians 4:8,9,16,17)

13

Poise Through Relaxation

Poise and relaxation go together like bread and butter and ham and eggs. You cannot maintain poise while you are tense. It is also true that you cannot relax and worry at the same time. Read the books, *Progressive Relaxation* and *You Must Relax,* by Dr. Edmund Jacobson.

Learn how to work under pressure without working under tension. This is possible if you have periodic breaks in your activities. That is, periodic rest periods. The rest may be a *change* in activity. It is only by this procedure that your heart continues to work for seventy years or so. And believe me, it *works*. It pumps enough blood through your body every twenty-four hours to fill a railway tanker. Every day it exerts as much effort as it would take to shovel twenty tons of gravel on to a platform as high as your waist. The reason it can do this incredible amount of work is because when it is beating moderately it works only nine hours out of twenty-four.

If you think to excuse your tension on the alleged (and fanciful) basis of your responsibilities, forget it! No one has had the responsibilities that fall upon our blessed Lord. If anyone had cause for tension, He had. Yet He always remained relaxed. Even when they sought to kill Him, He moved quietly and unhurriedly out of their midst. Can you possibly picture our Lord in a frenzied hurry? To be sure, however, there was a definiteness to His walk and to His talk and to the totality of His activities. He said,

> I must work the works of him that sent me, while it is day:
> The night cometh, when no man can work.   (John 9:4)

Yet despite that fact, on more than one occasion when pressured by others, He said in substance, "My opportunity is not yet come. The time is not fulfilled." He is our Exemplar in poise through relaxation. Hear Him as He says, "Come ye yourselves apart into a desert place, and rest a while . . ." (Mark 6:31).

Well did Vance Havner say, "The Lord told His disciples, 'Come ye apart and rest awhile.' What He meant was, 'Come ye apart and rest awhile or come ye apart.' " Well spoken words, Dr. Havner! It says that many were coming and going so they didn't have enough leisure to eat decently. You know some people think that they are busy when they are only nervous — rather, when they are only mentally maladjusted.

Now let us repeat J. B. Phillips' translation of verse 6:

> Don't worry over anything whatever; tell God every detail of your needs in earnest and thankful prayer, and the peace of God, which transcends human understanding, will keep constant guard over your hearts and minds as they rest in Christ Jesus.   (Philippians 4:6)

There is a rhythm, a cadence in all of nature. Plants reproduce themselves in their seasons and men in their generation. There is a rhythm, a cadence in all the action of nature — in our breathing, in the ebbing and flowing of the tide, in the rising and setting of the sun. One of the earmarks of the amateur musician is that he does not give proper observance to the rests.

Thomas Edison got by on four hours' sleep a day, we are told. However, he had the ability to "snooze" at almost any hour of the day or night. He was relaxed at all times. One of the most prominent of our contemporary psychologists has suggested that we need rest for the body and sleep for the mind. He goes on further to say that the man who stays free of psychic tensions gets by on less sleep than the man who gets tied up in knots.

The last year that Dr. Robert G. Lee was President of the Southern Baptist Convention he was in his sixties. During that year he traveled over 150,000 miles, built an auditorium that cost over one and a half million dollars, and received over 1200 new members into the 9,000-member Bellevue Baptist Church in Memphis, Tennessee, of which he was pastor.

One of his members, a prominent Memphis surgeon, Dr. J. Murray Davis, told me that the secret of Dr. Lee's output was his capacity to relax. Dr. Davis said, "It is incredible how this man maintains such a pace despite his years." Then the surgeon recounted this incident in the life of Dr. Lee. Said he, "One Sunday morning I went to make my hospital visits at six o'clock. Dr. Lee was also at the hospital visiting. He then taught our Sunday school class that morning and followed that by the delivery of one of his matchless sermons at the eleven o'clock hour. Immediately after the morning service he flew by chartered plane to Longview, Texas, where he delivered a baccalaureate address Sunday afternoon. He flew back to Memphis in time to speak at a special assembly of the Baptist Training Union in our Church. Following that he delivered the evening message at the seven-thirty evangelistic hour. After the benediction of the evening service he rushed to the airport where he boarded a plane for California. He flew all night and spoke Monday night to a large convocation in California." What a pace! Remember, this was when Dr. Lee was in his sixties.

For over a quarter of a century Dr. Lee averaged more than ten visits a day. He preached in his own church a minimum of three times a week and he taught a Sunday school class forty-four Sundays out of every year. After he was forty years of age he built a church from a membership of 1300 to a membership of more than 9,000 while all the time traveling and preaching outside his own city nearly as often as an evangelist. The secret? He knew how to relax! He knew how to pace himself! He worked under pressure without working under tension. Now in his eighties he probably preaches as often (if not more often) as any of our contemporary preachers.

Learn the rhythm of successful living. When you work, work. When you rest, rest.

When my father was sixty-two years of age he pastored a vigorous church in New York State. He slept only a few hours a night. He walked two miles a day. He was one of the best paddle ball players in Binghamton, New York, and all his opponents were under thirty-five. On his sixtieth birthday he played two sets of tennis. How did he do it? He knew how to relax. When visiting him the last time, I had an amusing experience. He was seated in his high-back rocking chair and I was seated across from him. Right in the middle of our conversation he said, "You must excuse me, son. I am going to take a few minutes' snooze." He laid his head back. I timed him. It was seven minutes. Opening his eyes and returning to his alert form, he said, "All right, now. Where were we?"

Most great achievers maintain the practice of having a nap sometime during the day. It has been proved that a person will fare better with six hours of sleep at night and an hour of sleep every afternoon than eight hours of sleep at night with no break in the day.

The soil of tension and frenzy is productive of the plant of worry. Therefore, ask God to help you to develop poise through relaxation.

14

Poise Through Scheduling

By scheduling your activities you will make great strides toward victory in the matter of relaxation.

Scheduling leads to relaxation because it defeats frenzy and hurry. Scheduling and regularity go together. These infer order and system which are the best antidotes to hurry. Hurry is symptomatic of a weak mind, or at least a weakly organized mind. Without scheduling and organization there is foolish haste which leads to glaring mistakes which in turn lead to discouragement and tension.

Let me suggest that you once again read the autobiography of Benjamin Franklin in which he tells of his effort to master the thirteen virtues. He was past eighty years of age when he wrote the autobiography and after passing the four-score-year mark he confided that order was the one virtue he had never been able to conquer. It is probably one of the most difficult habits to perfect.

Yet order is so important. Through disorganization we do not know where we are and there is always fear of the unknown. Worry, like a buzzard, preys upon the carrion of the disorganized mind.

I was told of a state hospital in Illinois. One day one of the inmates ran out of the gate and down the road as fast as he could run. The orderly chased him, caught him, and brought him back. The next day another inmate did exactly the same thing with the same result. That happened ten successive days with ten different inmates. Now, if the ten inmates had fled at the same time, and if each had run in a different direction, nine of them would have escaped. However, they were not *organized*. That's why they were in the institution!

Plan your work and work your plan. Ask God for the wisdom to help you plan your work and then ask God for the grace to enable you to work your plan. "The Lord is near." Call upon Him for the needed wisdom and grace.

Just as He led Nehemiah to plan for and to organize the work of the building of the wall around Jerusalem and just as He enabled Nehemiah and the brethren to work the plan — despite unspeakable opposition — so the Lord will enable you, if you will but call upon Him, to so plan your work and work your plan that you will fulfill the divine injunction to be "always abounding in the work of the Lord."

Fatigue is caused mostly by boredom. When you have no order — when you have failed to schedule your activities — you lack the awareness of accomplishment. Conversely, when you have wisely scheduled your activities under the leadership of the Holy Spirit, and when in His strength you are performing your responsibilities on schedule, you get the lift that comes from the awareness of accomplishment. There is nothing more invigorating than the knowledge of tasks efficiently completed and there is nothing more dispiriting than the knowledge of unfulfilled responsibilities.

Paul enjoins us to be "redeeming the time, for the days are evil." By His grace and in His strength we will fulfill our responsibility to redeem the time and at the same time we will conquer worry through poise by scheduling.

Korean Presbyterians invited me to be the evangelist in 1970 for the Seventh Decade Spiritual Revolution Crusade. The chairman was Dr. Kyung Chik Han, pastor of the world's largest Presbyterian Church . . . the Young Nak (meaning "eternal joy") Church in Seoul. The crusade was of three week's duration, with one week in each of three cities — Pusan, Taegu and Seoul.

For 21 days I was honored to be in the company of this world leader.

Twice dispossessed of all — literally *all* — his earthly goods, he had known the scourge of Japan's cruel occupation in the 40s and North Korea's atheistic terrorism in the 50s.

In 1956, with 27 North Korean refugees, Dr. Han founded the Young Nak Church. Just after the outer structure of the new sanctuary was completed, the North Koreans stormed across the 38th parallel and into Seoul, driving freedom-loving Koreans southward . . . and ultimately nearly into the sea. The new sanctuary was used by the North Koreans as an ammunition depot.

Dr. Han and his people established three other Young Nak churches during their southern exile.

Back in Seoul in 1953, the work continued, and the statistics are impressive. The membership climbed to more than 16,000 by 1972. More than 100 daughter churches were established. Schools, orphanages, senior citizens' quarters, summer camp and spiritual retreat grounds and facilities, special ministries among the military groups, are but a few of the projects launched under Dr. Han's leadership.

Yet, the dear man never appears harried or hurried. I watched for three weeks . . . in vain, I might add . . . for any sign of pique or impatience.

Dr. Han met with his people every morning for the 5 o'clock to 6 o'clock Dawn Prayer Meeting. What a way to start every day!

His life was and is a model of quiet achieveent . . . for Christ. He is the master teacher of "The Stewardship of Time." I have heard him. Better, I have watched him!

He so schedules himself, so plans his work and works his plan, that without frenzy he discharges herculean responsibilities.

He knows God has given him adequate time to achieve all that lies within the Divine will. In complete dependence upon

the Holy Spirit of God, he moves peacefully and productively.

Relaxed and gracious, he infuses a "God is in His heaven,
so fear not" mood into the room.

Dr. Han's life is a symphony of poise. The atmosphere of
his home is the vestibule to heaven. Fellowship with this man
of God bestows its own specia benediction.

The Lord gives us the ability and the time to do *everything*
He expects us to do. We have an obligation and privilege to
utilize these God-given resources to the end that His will for
us be fulfilled. Fulfillment of His will for us honors God and
tends to dispel worry.

God help us to be able to say as our Lord while yet on earth
could say:

> I have finished the work which thou gavest me to do.
>
> (John 17:4b)

15

Poise Through Sidelines

Probably a preferable word would be diversions. Beauty consists of contrasts, shades, varieties and changes. "Variety is the spice of life."

The Apostle Paul was not only a preacher; he was also a logician. Apparently he was interested in athletics, because he alluded to athletics many times in his epistles. Furthermore his reference to Greek poets in Acts 17 seems to indicate he was conversant with poetry. Certainly no one could deny that he was also a master psychologist.

David the king was a sportsman, a poet, a musician, a militarist, a philosopher. And who could adequately evaluate the multiplicity of interests maintained by his son Solomon?

> And he spake three thousand proverbs: and his songs were a thousand and five.
> And he spake of trees, from the cedar tree that is in Lebanon even unto the hyssop that springeth out of the wall: he spake also of beasts, and of fowl, and of creeping things, and of fishes. (1 Kings 4:32,33)

You will see here that Solomon was a sage — "he spake three thousand proverbs." He was a musician and poet — "and his songs were a thousand and five." He was an horticulturist — "and he spake of trees from the cedar tree that is in Lebanon even unto the hyssop that springeth out of the wall." He was an expert in animal husbandry — "he spake also of beasts." He was an ornithologist — "he spake of fowl." He was an entomologist — he spake "of creeping things." He was a piscatologist — he spake "of fishes."

Take the example of our own Lord. Study His parables and you will conclude that He was interested in and conversant with all phenomena and activities. Jesus was the Master Psychologist. He understood the laws of agriculture and horticulture. Our Lord displayed great interest in the sea and in fishing. He certainly understood the laws of anatomy and body function. He was an ornithologist and He knew animal husbandry.

Because of the broad interests of our Lord men of every strata of society and rank of individuality and echelon of culture listened to Him with absorption. He could appeal to the religious and cultured and educated Nicodemus equally as well as He could appeal to the woman of ill repute from Samaria.

Diversion of interests, a hobby, or an avocation effectuate the balance that leads to poise. They bring the other dimensions into life that give life real perspective.

When Paul the Apostle was forced out of Berea because of persecution and a threat to his life, he did not go to Athens and brood. He kept busy. In Athens he went down to the marketplace and listened to the dialogues of the philosophers. He studied the habit patterns of the Athenians. There he discovered their basic interests and their mental behavior. This turned out to be fruitful in the extreme. It wasn't long until they insisted that he go to Areopagus — to the top of Mars Hill — where only the great orators and the celebrities were permitted to speak. There he delivered the most masterful sermon ever preached by any man (our Lord excepted, of course). Through diversion he refused to give himself time to brood over his lot as a persecuted and a hounded preacher of the Word.

No man can honor God in a maximum way whose only

interests are within the boundaries of a narrow and specialized field. Without a variety of interests you will not maintain any interest for long.

You see, this works hand in glove with the already mentioned importance of becoming genuinely interested in other people.

The brilliant pulpit-orator from Louisiana, Dr. James W. Middleton, has been through enough to drive to despair and shatter the nerves of five rugged men. Recently he was out of his pulpit for nearly a year because of throat difficulties that subjected him to the surgeon's scalpel on two different occasions. His entire ministry seemed to be in jeopardy. Yet, as you listen to that matchless preacher, you are at once impressed with his poise — his sense of inner peace. As you hear that magnificently controlled bass voice rising and falling, whispering and roaring, declaiming and appealing, like a mighty four-manual pipe organ under the domination of a master, you detect complete mastery. I am convinced that one of the explanations of his self-control and poise lies in his hobbies, one of which is horticulture. He has performed some amazing grafts of plants in tree stumps. He, too, is a sportsman — a fisherman and a hunter of no mean ability.

Dr. Roy O. McClain, former pastor of the First Baptist Church of Atlanta, Georgia, and selected some years ago by *Time* as one of the ten outstanding American clergymen, had several hobbies, among which were the raising of Shetland ponies, painting, the playing of the organ, and woodworking. These hobbies served as a balance wheel enabling him to honor the Lord in a maximum way through unruffled poise even though he was saddled with the titanic task of pastoring the largest congregation in the State of Georgia.

I seriously doubt Australian Dr. Ernest Watson, dean of Haggai Institute, could maintain his Spirit-set pace were it not for the diversion he finds in swimming, music and other outside interests.

President Eisenhower found diversion in painting and in golf.

The late Dr. Harry A. Ironside, who was deprived of an

education past the eighth grade (I should say he was deprived of "schooling" past the eighth grade. His education was equivalent to that required to earn several doctor's degrees) found his diversion in poetry and in learning Greek and Chinese.

Dr. J. C. Massee, now deceased, formerly one of the nation's outstanding ministers, evangelists and seminary professors, maintained a youthfulness and a virility usually associated with a man half his years. He found diversion in the study of words and in gardening, to mention but two of his many interests. When I last talked with him, I was uplifted and challenged by his spirit. When many men at his age (the mid-eighties) would be complaining and dawdling, he was productively active. In discussing the blessings of the Lord upon his life, he said to me in a triumphant note, "My lines have fallen in pleasant places" (cf. Psalm 16:6).

You will notice that I have mentioned a number of clergymen. The reason for this is that ministers, more than any other group of men, have reason to get bogged down in the mire of routine responsibilities. They are on call twenty-four hours a day, seven days a week. They never have the satisfaction of knowing that everything is done. There is always another person to visit, another letter to write, another message to prepare. No wonder Dr. Wesley Schrader wrote the article appearing in *Life* some years ago on "Why Ministers Are Cracking Up."

Some women find diversion in mastering the art of cooking, in interior decorating, in gardening, in music, in writing, and in a host of other interests.

Let me suggest that for added stimulus along this line you read Marie Beynon Ray's book, *How Never to Get Tired*.

In Mark 6:31 when Jesus said to the apostles, "Come ye apart and rest awhile," the context shows that they did not go apart for a time of inactivity. Rather they went out to eat and then they engaged in a different form of activity. More times than not, rest is effectuated not by cessation of activity, but by change in the activity.

Jesus was always busy about His Father's business even

though the pattern of His activity changed often.

Some men, it is true, find within the framework of their calling enough variation so that they maintain the poise that comes through diversion within the confines of their calling. This was true of Dr. George W. Truett.

The world-famed industrialist, the late R. G. LeTourneau, had an important appointment in his plant at Toccoa, Georgia. While in flight to Georgia the landing gear of his plane stuck. The pilot radioed ahead to the Anderson, South Carolina, airport and told them of his plight. Ambulances and a rescue squad rushed to the airport. The newsmen and the cameramen were on the spot ready to cover the landing. They made a good crash landing. When Mr. LeTourneau got out of the plane his first words, in substance, were, "Where's the car? Where's the car? I am already late for my appointment in Toccoa. Can you get me a car immediately?"

There is poise. I asked him one time when he took his vacation. He said, "I never take a vacation. My work is my play and you never need a vacation from play." There was a man who through Christ and wise self-discipline learned the poise that conquers worry.

16

Poise Through Seizing the Day

In other words, live for today!

The songwriter D. W. Whittle understood this truth when he wrote,

> Moment by moment I'm kept in His love,
> Moment by moment I've help from above.
> Looking to Jesus, till glory doth shine;
> Moment by moment, Oh, Lord, I am thine.

The trouble with many people is that instead of "looking to Jesus" they are looking to tomorrow.

Yesterday is a cashed check and cannot be negotiated. Tomorrow is a promissory note and cannot be utilized today. Today is cash in hand. Spend it wisely.

> This is the day which the Lord hath made; we will rejoice and be glad in it. (Psalm 118:24)

Lowell Thomas had these words framed and hung on the walls of his broadcasting studio at his farm so that he could see them often.

If this verse is the conviction of your heart it is impossible for you to worry.

Don't live in the past. On the other hand, don't live in the future. Paul was in the habit of "forgetting those things which are behind'' (Philippians 3:13). While it is true that he was striving for future mastery, Philippians 3:12-14 makes it clear that his emphasis was on his opportunities and responsibilities during the present.

Give every moment your all. Give your entire attention to the work at hand, the person with whom you are talking or dealing. The Lord grants us time only in the quantity that we can use it — one moment at a time.

There is an illustration of our responsibility to live one day at a time in the story of the manna in Exodus 16. Now read this passage with special attention to the words that I have italicized.

> This is the thing which the Lord hath commanded, Gather of it every man *according to his eating, an omer for every man, according to the number of your persons* . . .
>
> And the children of Israel did so, and gathered, some more, some less.
>
> And when they did mete it with an omer, he that gathered much had nothing over, and he that gathered little had no lack; they gathered every man according to his eating.
>
> And Moses said, Let no man leave of it till the morning.
>
> Notwithstanding they hearkened not unto Moses; *but some of them left of it until the morning, and it bred worms, and stank:* . . .   (Exodus 16:16-20)

The Israelites were in need of food. The Lord provided for them a *daily* supply. He did not make available to them a week's supply. If they gathered more than a day's supply, all in excess of their daily requirements rotted. The truth is simply this: In the resources of God made available to you, *live for today*.

Here again our Lord is *the* example. He came to die. Through His death He would set up a kingdom — a kingdom not of this world, but a spiritual kingdom. Said Jesus, ''To this end was I born, and for this cause came I into the world'' (John 18:37).

The shadow of persecution and death constantly lay across His path. Nevertheless, He lived one day at a time and did not permit the grief, torture, and pain that faced Him to rob Him of perfect composure for today. Little children reveled in His company. Men who conversed with Him were aware of His total absorption with their own problems at that given time. Over and over again we can hear our Lord saying, "My hour is not yet come." In other words, He lived, "Moment by moment," one day at a time. Observe His matchless poise!

Don't be forever living in the future. As a Christian, look unceasingly for the Blessed Hope and Glorious Appearing of Jesus Christ, but while so doing, don't neglect your present work. Live in such a way that you would never be ashamed to meet Jesus no matter when He would appear.

In Acts 1:6 the followers of our Lord asked:

> Saying, Lord, wilt thou at this time restore again the kingdom to Israel?

Consider the answer of our Lord,

> . . . It is not for you to know the times or the seasons, which the Father hath put in his own power.
> But ye shall receive power, after that the Holy Ghost is come upon you: . . .   (Acts 1:7,8)

Our Lord replied by showing them that the finest possible preparation they could make for the future was a Spirit-led execution of the present. The proof that the child of God is looking forward to the Second Coming of Christ is made clear by his faithfulness in living *today* for the glory of God.

Montaigne said, "My life has been full of terrible misfortunes, most of which never happened." Many of us might say the same thing. How foolish of us to scuttle our opportunities and waste the privileges of this day which is slipping away with fantastic speed.

John Ruskin had on his desk a simple piece of stone on which was sculptured one word: *today*.

Osler gives good advice when he says, "Banish the future; live only for the hour and its allotted work . . . Set earnestly at the little task at your elbow . . . our plain duty is 'not to see what lies dimly at a distance, but to do what lies clearly at hand.' "

Yes, seize *today!* Richard Baxter left to us sage advice

when he said, "Spend your time in nothing which you know must be repented of; in nothing on which you might not claim the blessings of God; in nothing which you could not review with a quiet conscience on your dying bed; in nothing which you might not be safely and properly doing if guests surprise you in the act."

Most of your misery is left over from yesterday or borrowed from tomorrow. In the dynamic of the Holy Spirit determine to live today to the glory of God. This is the day that the Lord has made. Paul would remind you to redeem it (the time) for the days are evil (Ephesians 5:16). God has given you today. He has taken back all your yesterdays. All your tomorrows are still in His keeping.

The Lord graciously blessed us with a precious son. He was paralyzed and able to sit in his wheelchair only with the assistance of full-length body braces. One of the nation's most respected gynecologists and obstetricians brought him into the world. Tragically, this man — overcome by grief — sought to find the answer in a bourbon bottle rather than in a blessed Bible. Due to the doctor's intoxication at the time of delivery, he inexcusably bungled his responsibility. Several of the baby's bones were broken. His leg was pulled out at the growing center. Needless abuse — resulting in hemorrhaging of the brain — was inflicted upon the little fellow. (Let me pause long enough to say that this is no indictment upon doctors. I thank God for doctors. This man was a tragic exception. He was banned from practice in some hospitals, and, as mentioned previously, he committed suicide.)

During the first year of the little lad's life, eight doctors said he could not possibly survive. For the first two years of his life my wife had to feed him every three hours with a Brecht feeder. It took a half hour to prepare for the feeding and it took another half hour to clean up and put him back to bed. Not once during that time did she get out of the house for any diversion whatsoever. Never did she get more than two hours sleep at one time.

My wife, formerly Christine Barker of Bristol, Virginia, had once been acclaimed by some of the nation's leading musicians as one of the outstanding contemporary female vocalists in America. From the time she was thirteen she had been popular as a singer — and constantly in the public eye. Hers was the experience of receiving and rejecting some fancy offers with even fancier incomes to marry an aspiring Baptist pastor with no church to pastor!

Then, after five years of marriage, tragedy struck! The whole episode was so unnecessary. Eight of the nation's leading doctors said that our son could not survive. From a life of public service she was now marooned within the walls of our home. Her beautiful voice no longer enraptured public audiences with the story of Jesus, but was now silenced, or at best, muted to the subdued humming of lullabies.

Had it not been for her spiritual maturity whereby she laid hold of the resources of God and lived one day at a time, this heart-rending experience would long since have caused an emotional breakdown.

John Edmund, Jr., our little son, lived more than twenty years. We rejoice that he committed his heart and life to Jesus Christ and gave evidence of a genuine concern for the things of the Lord. I attribute his commitment to Jesus Christ and his wonderful disposition to the sparkling radiance of an emotionally mature, Christ-centered mother who has mastered the discipline of living one day at a time. Never have I — nor has anyone else — heard a word of complaint from her. The people who know her concur that at thirty-five years of age and after having been subjected to more grief than many people twice her age, she possessed sparkle that would be the envy of any high school senior and the radiance and charm for which any debutante would gladly give a fortune.

Seize today. Live for today. Wring it dry of every opportunity. You have troubles? So do others. So did Paul who said, "Most gladly therefore will I rather glory in my infirmities that the power of Christ may rest upon me" (2 Corinthians 12:9b).

A friend told me of his mother who worried for forty years that she would die of cancer. She died at seventy-three — *from pneumonia!* Tragic! She wasted forty years worrying *about the wrong thing*. Forty years she brought depression instead of delight to the hearts of her closest friends and members of her family. Forty years she divided her mind and her time between useful pursuits and worrying about cancer. Forty years her testimony for Christ was dimmed and her witness for Christ was diminished in power simply because she refused to live one day at a time — and to live that day to the fullest and to the glory of God.

Read it again:

> This is the day which the Lord hath made; we will rejoice and be glad in it. (Psalm 118:24)

17

Poise Through Skill

If you would develop the poise that conquers worry, do everything you do the best you can and learn to master some skill.

The late Dr. M. E. Dodd well said, "Many are twisting a tune out of a hand organ when they ought to be playing a four-manual pipe organ. Many are satisfied to play with mud pies when they ought to be making angel food cakes. Many are crawling when they ought to be running. Many are building shacks when they ought to be building palaces."

First Corinthians 10:31 says:

> Whether therefore ye eat, or drink, or whatsoever ye do, do all to the glory of God.

Therefore if we are going to glorify God, we must do our best. There is no room for mediocrity in the life of the child of God. God deserves and demands our best.

> Hear ye the Master's call, "Give Me thy best!"
> For, be it great or small, That is His test.
> Do then the best you can, Not for reward,
> Not for the praise of men, But for the Lord.
>
> Wait not for men to laud, Heed not their slight;
> Winning the smile of God Brings its delight!

Aiding the good and true Ne'er goes unblest,
All that we think or do, Be it the best.

Night soon comes on a pace, Day hastens by;
Workman and work must face Testing on high.
Oh, may we in that day Find rest, sweet rest,
Which God has promised those Who do their best.

Every work for Jesus will be blest,
But He asks from everyone His best.
Our talents may be few, These may be small,
But unto Him is due Our best, our all.

Skill is essential to poise. The speaker who has subjected himself to rigorous discipline until he has perfected the craft of speaking is poised when he speaks. The speaker who has not paid the price of discipline and who comes to the pulpit or to the lectern half-prepared lacks poise. If he has any discernment he is tortured at the conclusion of his message as he reflects upon the mess he made of it. The anxiety produced thereby is totally unnecessary and could have been eliminated if he had simply paid the price in developing the needed skill. The same is true of the doctor, the lawyer, the salesman, the artisan, the athlete, the artist, the cook.

For a professing Christian to do less than his best is inexcusable. The Christian has the motive and has the resources for mastery available.

Tragic it is that there are few great musicians today. Few great orators. Few great financiers. Few great inventors. Thank God, however, there are still some who are willing to soar to the heights of the eagle though they know they will fly alone. For the glory of God and for their own peace of mind they are willing to climb the ladder of achievement even though they know that thorns on the rungs will pierce their feet.

Some time ago I had an interview with one of the greatest speech professors in America. He showed me seven pages of elementary voice exercises which, to my amazement, he said he has practiced daily for forty years. This man cannot tolerate mediocrity.

Paderewski practiced simple finger exercises for hours

every day over a period of years. No wonder the musical world was hypnotized into the realm of ecstacy by the charm of his musical mastery.

Edison experimented multiplied hundreds of times before he successfully developed the electric light filament. While he was working on it a scientist in England said that anyone was a fraud who would say the electric light filament was a possibility. But Thomas Edison, who loathed mediocrity, kept on giving his best until success crowned his efforts.

Matthew Henry worked hours every day for forty years in producing his *Commentaries*. They probably appear on the bookshelves of more clergymen than any other commentary. Why? Because, under God, Matthew Henry gave his best.

Jesus told the parable of the man who started the house but never lived in it. Our Master scorned a task half-done.

William Jennings Bryan for years unrelentingly, tediously, laboriously practiced the art of oratory. He never won a speech contest. Nevertheless he kept on. As a comparative unknown he attended the Democratic National Convention held at the Coliseum in Chicago in 1896. Here the years of self-denial and self-discipline paid off. It was past midnight. The people were weary. Many of them were leaving. He stepped up to the stand and delivered his famous *Cross of Gold* oration. This oration so masterfully delivered by the man who never won a speech contest catapulted him into the position of standard-bearer for the Democratic party. In less than twenty-four hours he had become a national figure. This mighty man of God had mastered the mechanics of the work for which God had called him and the record of his life is a glittering trophy and an imposing monument to the glory of God.

Peace of mind is dependent upon the awareness of divine approval. When we fail to give God our best, we fail to bring maximum honor and glory to His name. The consciousness of this failure produces anxiety and inner conflict.

There is no poise like the poise that accompanies the knowledge of mastery to the glory of God — mastery effectuated in the power of God.

Whatever may be your personal appraisal of television, I think you must confess with me that it presents one of the most stinging rebukes to the apathy of church leadership. Performers will work day and night to attain mastery in the field of show business. Some time ago, when Kate Smith was on TV, I read that for every hour that she was on TV she spent eighteen hours in preparation. At that time she was on five hours a week. For five hours of TV entertainment she willingly worked ninety hours to bring to her viewers the finest programs of which she was capable. She did not have to do this for monetary reasons, for she is reputedly a millionaire several times over.

On the other hand, consider how shoddily we treat the Lord, and by "we" I am referring to professing Christians. Take an example. A soloist gets up to sing. Possibly he has rehearsed that particular number, but more probably he hasn't. He sticks his nose in the crease of the book and has to read every word. Imagine an opera star bound down to script and music! What conclusion do you come to? Yes, that's right. The opera star apparently is more devoted to the mastery of his profession than the average gospel soloist is to the glory of God.

In Philippians 4:13 Paul assures us:

> I can do all things through Christ which strengtheneth me.

You have the resources necessary to do what God requires of you. And in the fulfillment of His requirement you will have poise that conquers anxiety.

We like to do what we know how to do well. You are less likely to worry while you are doing what you like to do. Worry results from a divided mind. When you are doing what you like to do, your mind is occupied with one thing. "This one thing I do," said Paul. Dwight L. Moody said most people would have to alter that and confess, "These fifty things I dabble in."

The high school boy enjoys that sport most which he plays best. The housewife is contentedly happy when in the process of making a cake for which she is famous in the community.

Watch Leonard Bernstein on television. For one solid hour he holds a capacity studio audience of hundreds of children spellbound and charms millions of television viewers. He is totally absorbed. Obviously he enjoys it. Why? Because he is probably the world's greatest music teacher when it comes to explaining music to the masses. He apparently likes to do this because he has mastered the skill of doing it well. At the conclusion of the hour, even the television viewers detect that he is nearly exhausted, but supremely happy. Yes, I might add, he is poised.

Our high school principal, who also taught us American History, admonished us over and over again to "learn to do at least one thing better than anyone else can do it."

Have you not had this experience many times? Perhaps it was at a party, or maybe a picnic. You saw someone who seemed absolutely bored — thoroughly disgusted. That individual moped around on the sidelines, refusing to participate in the activities. Then, a game or a sport was proposed, the mention of which brought light into his eyes. He threw himself into that game, into that sport, with everything he had. He was skillful in that activity. Now his body was vibrant. His countenance scintillated. His conversation was spirited. Why? Simply because he was now poised. He was skilled in the particular activity and became congenially involved in the group. His mind was no longer divided. His interests were no longer diffused. Obviously he was supremely happy. The explanation simply lies in the fact that we enjoy doing what we know how to do well.

If you would conquer worry, discipline yourself to the point of mastery in the field to which God has called you. It is also well for you to become competent in some other fields. This will redound to God's glory, your happiness and other people's profit.

Jeremiah says:

> Cursed be he that doeth the work of the Lord deceitfully, (the margin renders it "negligently") and cursed be he that keepeth back his sword from blood.   (Jeremiah 48:10)

For your own peace of mind excel in at least one thing. Concentrate all your forces upon some work. Gather in your resources, rally all your faculties, marshal all your energies, focus all your capacities upon mastery in at least one field of endeavor. This is a sure-fire antidote to the divided mind. Stop scattering your fire. Cease any half-hearted interests to be superb in everything. Ascertain the will of God for your life. Enlist His help and strength through whom you can do all things. Strive for mastery, and experience worry-killing poise through skill.

18

Poise Through Industry

When you are idle you are subject to destructive thoughts, dangerous impulses, and perilous pressures from without. All these things contribute to anxiety.

Jesus Himself said, "I must work" (John 9:4). Jesus also said, "My Father worketh hitherto and I work" (John 5:17).

Work is divine in its inception. The old adage, "Idleness is the devil's workshop," is true.

Reflect upon the grief that idleness brought David the king. When he should have been in battle, he was home taking it easy. While idling about his palace he saw a sight which stirred his sexual passions. Still idle, he reflected and meditated upon that experience until it festered into the open sin of covetousness and then adultery. Those sins in turn led to the murder of Uriah, the husband of Bathsheba. Before long the entire affair was public knowledge. Talk about anxiety! I have no doubt that David at one point would gladly have died rather than lived through the grief and anxiety produced by the harvest of his idleness.

Paul the Apostle had been pursued by hostility at Berea, and it was necessary for him to flee to Athens — alone! In Athens he could have holed up in some private room and felt sorry for himself. He could have brooded over the mistreatment he had suffered for the work of the Lord. He could have said, "I have been laboring night and day in Thessalonica and preaching faithfully in Berea. Now I will take it easy." Not Paul. Immediately he began an investigation of conditions in Athens. After acquainting himself with the conditions in this intellectual metropolis, he began to preach in the synagogue with the Jews and with devout persons in the marketplace daily. Soon his ministry attracted the interest of the philosophers, of the Epicureans, and of the Stoics. They requested a speech from him in which he would set forth his philosophy. He could have responded, "Oh, no. I was stoned and left for dead at Lystra. I was beaten and jailed in Philippi. I have just now been abused in Berea for this very thing — preaching the Gospel of the Son of God, whom I serve." Paul was not of this stripe, however. Far from feeling sorry for himself, he shared with them this blessed Gospel. At their behest he walked up the stone steps to the top of Areopagus, the ancient judgment seat of Athens where in the crescent of stone seats had sat the judges who 300 years previously had condemned Socrates to die. Here this ambassador of the Judge of the earth delivered probably the greatest sermon ever to come from the lips of mortal man.

Thorough preparation was an essential characteristic of Paul's ministry. As soon as God had saved him in Damascus, he immediately started preparation in Arabia and then in Jerusalem, developing skill (consider this against the backdrop of the preceding chapter) in the work for which God had called him. He was speaking to the intellectuals of the world. The laws of this city pronounced death upon anyone introducing a foreign deity. Did that stop Paul? He was a Jewish tentmaker, "whose bodily presence is weak and whose speech is of no account," but he spoke out in that classic and proud city of the ancient world.

It was in the marketplace at Athens that Socrates, "the wisest" of men, asked his immortal questions. Over in the nearby olive groves by the brook, Plato founded his academy. To the east was the Lyceum of Aristotle. Near at hand in the Agora were the garden of Epicureans and the painted porch of the Stoics. Here was the home of the drama where the scholars spoke with pride the names of Aeschylus and Sophocles. Here spoke the orators of Greece. Here were historians like Thucydides and Xenaphon. In their Athenian temples the national spirit of Athens was deified in the marble images of their heroes and soldiers, in the trophies of her victories, in her multifarious objects of interest. Here Paul introduced a foreign deity — God Almighty.

Here Paul preached:

The personality of God
The self-existence of God
The omnipotence of God
The unity of God
The reality of divine providence
The universality of divine providence
The efficiency of divine providence
The spirituality of divine worship
The nonexternality of divine worship
The unity of the human race
The brotherhood of the human race
The possibility of a true natural religion
The dignity of man
The dependence of man
The absurdity of idols and idol worship
The essential graciousness of God's dealings with the race of man
The duty of immediate repentance
The certainty of a day of judgment
The exaltation of Jesus Christ to the office of supreme judge
The reality of a future life.

Here Paul corrected the errors of:

Atheism, or the dogma that there is no God
Pantheism, or the theory that all is God
Materialism, or the notion that the world is eternal
Fatalism, or the superstition that no intelligence presides over the universe, but all things come to pass either by necessity or chance

Polytheism, or the fancy that there are or can be many gods

Ritualism, or the imagination that God can be honored by purely external performances

Evolutionism, or the hypothesis that man is a product of force and of matter

Indifferentism, or the creed that man should seek after nothing and no one higher than himself

Optimism, or the delusion that this is the best possible world and man has no sin of which to repent

Unitarianism, or the tenet that Christ was an ordinary member of the race

Annihilationism, or the belief that after death there is nothing

Universalism, or the sentiment that all will be saved.

Talk about skill! Talk about mastering one's field! What discipline!

The development of this skill required great industry, and Paul had learned the wisdom of industry. He was always engaged in some worthwhile pursuit. Because of his diligence, God was pleased to open up to him doors of opportunity. As a result of the effective execution of his opportunity, God blessed his ministry and at the same time delivered him from fear and anxiety. "I know both how to be abased and I know how to abound" (Philippians 4:12).

He was so busy he had no time for fear-producing, worry-loaded thoughts!

Paul refused to worry even though he was imprisoned in Rome. Read 2 Timothy 4:13. He makes request of Timothy to bring the "books, but especially the parchments." Industry! This mighty man of God remained industrious right to the end.

Many people piously assert that they are bound "to wait upon the Lord" and to "trust in the Lord" while they sit on the stool of do-nothing, twiddle their thumbs, and piously pretend to be waiting for the Lord's return. Now it is true that we must "wait upon the Lord" and "trust in the Lord." Nevertheless, the proof that we are waiting upon the Lord and trusting in the Lord will be revealed in our "always abounding in the work of the Lord" (1 Corinthians 15:58).

By industry I refer to activity with a worthwhile purpose and toward a worthwhile goal. This is essential to the poise that conquers worry since you cannot fasten your mind upon two things at once. You cannot throw all your energies into God-glorifying activity while at the same time focusing your attention upon fear-producing thoughts.

Death is characterized by inaction, life by action. As death approaches, action decreases. It can also be proved that decreasing activity hastens death. Do you not know some who were in good health until their retirement and then it seemed as though immediately their health began to break and death seemed to run toward them like Mercury with wings at his heels?

There are some who would rationalize their idleness by their advanced years. Don't think to immunize yourself from the responsibility to industry simply because you are advanced in years.

Commodore Vanderbilt built most of his railroads when he was well over seventy, making his hundreds of millions at an age when most men have retired.

Kant wrote some of his greatest philosophical works when he was past seventy.

Goethe wrote the second part of Faust after he was eighty and Victor Hugo was still astounding the world with some of his finest writings after his eightieth birthday.

Tennyson was eighty-three when he wrote "Crossing the Bar."

Benjamin Franklin most helped his country after he was sixty.

Palmerston was Premier of England at eighty-one, Gladstone at eighty-three. Bismarck was vigorously administering the affairs of the German Empire at seventy-four. Christy was Premier of Italy at seventy-five.

Verdi wrote operas after he was eighty.

Titian painted his incomparable "Battle of Lepanto" at ninety-eight, his "Last Supper" at ninety-nine.

Michelangelo was producing masterpieces in the field of sculpture at eighty-nine.

Monet was painting great masterpieces after eighty-five.

I believe that one of the outstanding factors contributing to the longevity of Sir Winston Churchill and General Douglas MacArthur was the fact that they both knew and utilized the value of industry.

Men like these mentioned don't have time for anxiety. Worry is a time thief and they refuse to be robbed by it.

Charles Haddon Spurgeon, the famous London preacher of a century ago, well said that "it seems that some people are industriously asleep and lazily awake."

Many parents sin against their children in our day by instilling into them the habit of idleness. Today it seems we must bribe our children to run errands, reimburse them for washing behind their ears, and give them a bonanza for passing their grades. In so treating them we are producing a condition that will inevitably lead to anxiety and frustration in later life. Even at twelve years of age our Lord, when sought by His parents, responded, "Wist ye not that I must be about my Father's business?" (Luke 2:49).

19

Poise Through Stewardship

In talking about stewardship now I am referring to material possessions. I realize that stewardship involves time and talents, as well.

No man has a right to expect blessings from God if he through greed and covetousness blocks the pathway down which God's blessings march.

God is the owner of all things. We are stewards. God knew that man would contest this fact and so He went to special pains to make His ownership clear in the opening chapters of the Bible. God's name is mentioned fourteen times in the first thirteen verses, thirty-one times in the first chapter, and forty-five times in the first two chapters of Genesis.

God requires stewardship not because of His need, but rather because of our need. He has no need.

> For every beast of the forest is mine, and the cattle upon a thousand hills.
>
> If I were hungry, I would not tell thee: for the world is mine, and the fulness thereof.   (Psalm 50:10,12)
>
> The silver is mine, and the gold is mine, saith the Lord of hosts.   (Haggai 2:8)

God has a threefold basis for demanding our stewardship.

Read Isaiah 43:1:

> But now thus saith the Lord that created thee, O Jacob, and
> he that formed thee, O Israel, Fear not: for I have redeemed
> thee, I have called thee by thy name; thou art mine.

He created us, He redeemed us. He sustains us.

It is impossible for a man to experience the poise that
conquers worry unless he possesses an awareness of the
approval of God. Without the awareness of divine approval,
man is plagued by feelings of guilt and consequent fears. He
may be a Hottentot in Africa, or a man-eating savage from the
South Sea Islands. He may be totally uncivilized; but as a
result of that monitor God has placed in his breast, man
knows that he is responsible to a higher power. Not until he
comes to know this higher power — God Almighty —
personally through the mediation of Jesus Christ, is his guilt
resolved and do his fears subside.

Many are foolishly trying to get victory over guilt and fear
by the utilization of Freudian expressionism and catharsis,
Gestalt formulae, positive thinking, and the like. However it
is only God who banishes our fear and through the instrumen-
tality of the Holy Spirit gives us the spirit "of power, and of
love, and of a sound mind" (2 Timothy 1:7).

It is possible for a Christian to be out of fellowship with
God and thus forfeit this poise that is dependent upon our
awareness of His approval.

God has set forth certain principles which transcend the
boundaries of time segments, geographical divisions and
race groups. One principle God set down was the principle
regarding time which He made eloquently clear in the first
chapter of the Bible. One day out of seven belongs to Him.
This principle has never changed, though it has been disobeyed and denied and abused. God has never rescinded this
requirement.

Another principle that transcends time is the principle
regarding the doctrine of substitutionary sacrifice as the only
answer to man's sin. When Abel offered an atoning sacrifice
it was in response to this fundamental law — this unalterable

principle. Hebrews 11:4 tells us that Abel offered the sacrifice "by faith" meaning that there had been a revelation from God concerning it. Now all sacrifices have had their fulfillment in Christ, "the Lamb of God which taketh away the sin of the world" (John 1:29).

The third fundamental law — unalterable principle — is that relating to the stewardship of material possessions.

Attention! If you are inclined to get a little impatient with this emphasis on stewardship and turn over to the next chapter, I implore you to hear me out — or rather hear God's Word out. One out of every six verses of the four gospels has to do with the right and wrong use of material possessions and sixteen of our Lord's thirty-eight parables have to do with the right and wrong use of material possessions. Don't sin against yourself by ignoring this chapter. Suspend your judgment and "to thine own self be true." Surely more anxiety, worry and divided-mindedness among Christians is caused by deficiency at this point than at any other.

In the Garden of Eden God kept to Himself the tree of knowledge of good and evil. This He did to remind Adam and Eve of their stewardship and of God's ownership. They were not to touch the fruit of that tree. That belonged to God in a special sense. True, everything belongs to God, but a certain proportion of that which He bestows upon us is to be set aside immediately and with no strings attached.

Is not the tenant farmer in the Midwest required to give back to the owner one-fourth of the corn crop? Is not the tenant farmer in the South required to give back to the landowner one-third of the cotton crop? Since God is the owner of all things, is it not fair that we be required to give back to Him a proportion of that which He makes possible?

Remember verse 5 of our text in Philippians 4. The word *moderation* means "fairness" among other things. There is no poise without fairness and there is no fairness without stewardship of material possessions. This poise that brings peace is significantly dependent upon our obedience to stewardship opportunities.

The most impelling incentive to give is not to provide the

church with financial resources. The child of God *pays* his tithe and *gives* offerings over and above the tithe "as the Lord hath prospered him":

(1) In recognition of God's sovereign ownership

> But thou shalt remember the Lord thy God: for it is he that giveth thee power to get wealth, that he may establish his covenant which he sware unto thy fathers, as it is this day.
>
> (Deuteronomy 8:18)

> What? know ye not that your body is the temple of the Holy Ghost which is in you, which ye have of God, and ye are not your own?
>
> For ye are bought with a price: therefore glorify God in your body, and in your spirit, which are God's.
>
> (1 Corinthians 6:19,20)

(2) In appreciative acknowledgment of redeeming grace

> For by grace are ye saved through faith; and that not of yourselves: it is the gift of God:
>
> Not of works, lest any man should boast.
>
> For we are his workmanship, created in Christ Jesus unto *good works,* which God hath before ordained *that we should walk in them.*
>
> (Ephesians 2:8-10)

(3) In surrender of life and talents to the Lord

> I beseech you therefore, brethren, by the mercies of God, that ye present your bodies a living sacrifice, holy, acceptable unto God, which is your reasonable service.
>
> And be not conformed to this world; but be ye transformed by the renewing of your mind, that ye may prove what is that good, and acceptable, and perfect, will of God.
>
> (Romans 12:1,2)

When you prepare your tithe you prepare for worship. In church as you put the money in the collection plate you are saying in substance, "This is a tangible expression of my total surrender to Thee. This money that I place in this plate represents my brains, my blood, my abilities — all of the blessings that have come from Thee, for I realize that

> Every good gift and every perfect gift is from above, and cometh down from the Father of lights, with whom is no variableness, neither shadow of turning.   (James 1:17)

It is because of the health, because of the mental ability, because of the friends, because of the various resources that Thou hast given me that I am able to make a living. All that I am and all that I have is Thine. My stewardship of material possessions is but an expression of that fact.''

The basis of our monetary responsibility is the tithe. Tithing is paying back to God 10 percent of the increase. God says that if you fail to pay that 10 percent back into the ''storehouse'' with faithful regularity you are a thief and a robber.

There are those who would try to brainwash people into believing that the responsibility of the tithe was only in force during the days of the law — from the time of Moses to the time of Christ. They will tell you that Malachi 3:10 has no relevance for today because it is in the Old Testament. The Lord must have known that such mischief would be attended. Therefore He introduced the words of Malachi 3:6, ''For I am the Lord, I change not. . . .'' (Malachi 3:6). After these words He calls Israel back to His ordinances, to tithes and offerings, to the storehouse, and to His conditional promise of blessing. The New Testament reaffirms these words of Malachi 3:6 by saying that with God there is ''no variableness, neither shadow of turning.''

These same people who say that tithing was for those under the law turn to Psalm 23 for comfort, to Psalm 32 for guidance, to Job for wisdom, and comfort in trials and tribulations, to Elijah for a pattern of prayer, and to other Old Testament passages for leadership.

To be consistent these people who would throw out Malachi 3:10 ought also to throw out John 3:16 because it, too, was spoken prior to the time that redemption was completed by our Lord on the Cross of Calvary.

Tithing antedated the law. Abraham tithed. The law of the tithe is not an Israelitish law. It is a fundamental and unalterable law of God. It is still in force. That is why tithing is commended by Jesus.

Woe unto you, scribes and Pharisees, hypocrites: for *ye pay tithe* of mint and anise and cummin, and have omitted the weightier matters of the law, judgment, mercy, and faith: these ought ye to have done, and *not to leave the other undone*. (Matthew 23:23)

Just as Abraham paid tithes to Melchizedek so we pay tithes to Christ. In Hebrews 7 this truth is made clear. The Son of God who liveth and abideth a priest continually after the order of Melchizedek "receiveth tithes" — receives them now! When paying tithes, Abraham acknowledged Melchizedek's sovereignty for he was a king-priest. Likewise today when one pays his tithe he acknowledges Christ as his Sovereign, his Lord. Refusal to pay the tithe is refusal to own Christ as Sovereign and as one's High Priest. Thus one makes Christ not only inferior to Melchizedek, but also inferior to the Levites, the priestly group of Old Testament times.

The tithe was incorporated in the law. This was done because it was a principle worthy of divine enforcement. God never repealed the fundamental law of tithing; grace has not annulled it; time has not altered it.

Tithing was commanded by Malachi.

> Will a man rob God? Yet ye have robbed me. But ye say, Wherein have we robbed thee? In tithes and offerings.
>
> Ye are cursed with a curse: for ye have robbed me, even this whole nation.
>
> Bring ye all the tithes into the storehouse, that there may be meat in mine house, and prove me now herewith, saith the Lord of hosts, if I will not open you the windows of heaven, and pour you out a blessing, that there shall not be room enough to receive it.
>
> And I will rebuke the devourer for your sakes, and he shall not destroy the fruits of your ground; neither shall your vine cast her fruit before the time in the field, saith the Lord of hosts.
>
> And all nations shall call you blessed: for ye shall be a delightsome land, saith the Lord of hosts.
>
> (Malachi 3:8-12)

In this command Malachi makes the practice of tithing essential to receiving blessings of a superior nature and to a degree and in a measure not otherwise promised.

This passage in Malachi teaches that when a man refuses to tithe he is: (1) guilty of robbing God, (2) subjected to a curse, and (3) denied the right of the blessings of God.

Grace does not abrogate the law. Grace fulfills the law — and goes much further than the most stringent demands of the law. Grace provides the dynamic necessary for fulfilling the law's mechanics. The law told man what to do, but failed to provide him with the capability to accomplish it. Grace provides the dynamic of the Holy Spirit whereby in the strength of God man fulfills the demands of the law — and much more.

Jesus said in Matthew 5:17-20:

> Think not that I am come to destroy the law, or the prophets: I am not come to destroy, but to fulfill.
>
> For verily I say unto you, Till heaven and earth pass, one jot or one tittle shall in no wise pass from the law, till all be fulfilled.
>
> Whosoever therefore shall break one of these least commandments, and shall teach men so, he shall be called the least in the kingdom of heaven: but whosoever shall do and teach them, the same shall be called great in the kingdom of heaven.
>
> For I say unto you, That except your righteousness shall exceed the righteousness of the scribes and Pharisees, ye shall in no case enter into the kingdom of heaven.

Already in this chapter it has been pointed out that Jesus commended the tithing of the Pharisees. In verse 20 of Matthew 5, the Lord tells us that our righteousness must *exceed* the righteousness of the Scribes and Pharisees. Grace fulfills and amplifies instead of destroying and minimizing the law.

Proceed further in Matthew 5. The law says, "Thou shalt not kill." Jesus makes it clear that if a man hates his brother he is just as guilty as if he had murdered him. The law said, "Thou shalt not commit adultery." Jesus points out that under grace whosoever looks on a woman to lust after her has already violated the seventh commandment in his heart.

Carry this principle over in the matter of the stewardship of money. How can an enlightened child of God do less under grace than the Jew did under the law? The Jew gave offerings over and above his tithe, too. For instance, if you will study the Old Testament you will discover that the Temple and the equipage thereof were paid for by offerings over and above the tithes. There is always a question mark in my mind about that person who goes to such extremes to prove that we are under no obligation to tithe. What is his motive?

In Leviticus 27:30 God makes it clear that, "The tithe is the Lord's." Therefore we, as stewards, have absolutely no right to handle it as though it were ours. It must be placed where God says and when God says. Namely, in the storehouse on the Lord's Day.

Jesus said, "Render therefore unto Caesar the things which are Caesar's; and unto God the things that are God's" (Matthew 22:21).

In other words, pay your taxes and pay your tithes. Your taxes belong to the government. The proof of this lies in the fact that they are deducted from your pay before you receive it. Your United States income tax is to be paid to the Collector of Internal Revenue at a given location.

Suppose you owed the government an income tax of a thousand dollars. Suppose that you made out your 1040 Form and attached a note to it in which you said:

> Dear Uncle Sam,
>
> You will notice that I owe you a thousand dollars. I am sending $100 to my local postmaster. He is one of your faithful servants and he is having a hard time financially. I am sending $100 to a U.S.O. down in South Carolina. They are doing a magnificent work boosting the morale of your own servicemen and they need help desperately. I am sending $100 to a nephew of mine who is a sailor with the Seventh Fleet. He is liable to get blown up any time and I think that he needs encouragement. After all, he is one of your faithful servicemen. Then I am sending $200 to the Veterans Ad-

ministration. After all, they are loyally dedicated to carrying out your will. *But,* Uncle Sam, just to let you know my heart is in the right place, I am sending the remaining $500 to the Collector of Internal Revenue in my area here.

"Absurd," you say. Why? Simply because no man would survive this miscarriage of responsibility with impunity.

Here is a man who owes God a tithe of a thousand dollars. But instead of accepting God's revelation that, "The tithe is the Lord's," he says, "The tithe is mine. My tithe!" Then, acting on that premise he high-handedly determines the distribution of that money which is not his in the first place. He will send $100 to a radio evangelist, another $100 to a Bible school, and another $100 to a missionary. The tithe is to go into the storehouse, which in this age is the church. *All the tithe is to go into the storehouse*.

Hear the Word of the Lord:

> Upon the first day of the week let every one of you lay by him in store, as God hath prospered him, that there be no gatherings when I come.   (1 Corinthians 16:2)

> Bring ye all the tithes into the storehouse, that there may be meat in mine house, and prove me now herewith, saith the Lord of hosts, if I will not open you the windows of heaven, and pour you out a blessing, that there shall not be room enough to receive it.   (Malachi 3:10)

The same word that is translated "store" in 1 Corinthians 16:2 is the word used in the Septuagint translation and translated "storehouse" in Malachi 3:10. In other words, it would be a correct translation of 1 Corinthians 16:2 to say, "Upon the first day of the week let every one of you lay by him in storehouse . . ."

These scriptural truths are set forth by one who doesn't pastor a local church. Rather, he leads up a para-church organization dependent upon the gifts of God's people.

Gifts over and above the tithe can be made to Christian causes. But "the tithe is the Lord's." The specific depository is the local church, and it is to be placed there undesignated.

In 1957, when the Lord led me to resign the pastorate to go

into the field of evangelism, a dear friend who fought this truth said, "Haggai, now I reckon you will abandon this foolishness about storehouse tithing."

"My change in ministry doesn't mean a change in Scripture or commitment," I replied.

"Follow that notion, and in a year you will collapse for lack of support," he insisted.

Said I, "If this ministry is of God, He'll supply the need."

It was, and He has.

When a man refuses to storehouse tithe his money, he is repeating in kind — if not in degree — the sin of Adam and Eve. They took to themselves an authority that was not theirs in partaking of the forbidden fruit. That tree belonged to God, not to them. When a man does not tithe, he is taking to himself an authority that is not his in appropriating to himself money that belongs to God. How then can he expect peace? How can he expect victory over anxiety and freedom from worry? For God and God alone is the Author of peace.

Here is a man who will not honor God with the payment of the tithe. However, when his little child becomes critically ill, and the doctors say there is no hope apart from supernatural intervention, that same father will fall on his face before God and in substance will say, "O God, this is my child, bone of my bones, flesh of my flesh, blood of my blood. I hand him to Thee. Do what seems good in Thy sight. If it can please Thee, restore him to health and strength and to us." Such hypocrisy! He is willing to trust God with his own flesh and blood! Even this man who is not willing to trust God with his filthy silver and gold? Does he think more of his money than he does of his child? Do you see the hypocrisy of it, dear friend? How can God honor a man like this? How can God in justice bless a man like this who turns his back upon God when he so desires — yes, turns his back upon God every time he refuses to tithe.

Yet another illustration. You will remember the passage in Mark 12:41-44. Jesus sat over against the treasury and beheld how the people cast money into the treasury. You will remember, also, that a certain poor widow put in two mites. Jesus called his disciples together, and said, "This poor widow hath cast more in than all they which have cast into the treasury." How could He know? Perhaps they had put part of their tithe into a religious foundation, or some Bible college, or sent it to some radio evangelist. You say, they didn't have such things back then! That's true, but let me hasten to add, it is a fact of history that there were more depositories for the giving of alms in that day than there are today. The others could have said they had given much of the tithe to alms' depositories. Jesus judged their stewardship on the basis of what they put into the treasury of the house of God which today is our own literal, visible, local church.

Consider the process of bringing the tithe: (1) *Bring* the tithe. This couples tithing with worship. The two are inseparable. (2) Bring *all* the tithe. Don't deduct your doctor's bills, your transportation to and from work, your insurance policies, your gifts to the Red Cross, United Appeal Drive, and so forth. Bring a full 10 percent of your total increase. (3) Bring ye all the tithe into the *storehouse*. When this is done your responsibility ceases. Even when Paul was trying to get money together for Jerusalem he didn't tell the Corinthian Christians to send their tithe there. He told them to put their tithe in their local church and then he urged the church itself to help out the church in Jerusalem.

Now notice the conditional promise of Malachi 3:10:

> And prove me now herewith, saith the Lord of hosts, if I will not open you the windows of heaven, and pour you out a blessing, that there shall not be room enough to receive it.

Let us add, also, verses 11 and 12.

If I could not believe what God says about tithing, I could not believe what He says about anything. Strange it is that people will believe what He says about salvation, what He says about heaven, what He says about hell, what He says about baptism, what He says about soul-winning — yet they will not believe what He says about tithing and the stewardship of possessions.

I know a wealthy man who has set up a religious foundation. He allegedly puts in 10 percent of his earnings into that foundation and therefore considers himself a tither. However, he does not put the tithe where God says to put it. In addition to that manifest disobedience, one of his corporations borrows the money that is in the nonprofit religious foundation — borrows it at the rate of six percent. Therefore he has access to money on which he has to pay no tax — money that he uses to expand his business. You say, "Well, preacher, God is blessing him." Is He? The trouble is that too many people think only in terms of money when they think of God's opening the windows of heaven and pouring out blessings.

I know a man who made $40 million last year, but because of an ulcerated stomach he can't eat a decent piece of meat. There are some men who would give all of their money if they could buy peace of mind, the respect of their children, the love of their wife.

Once again, let me remind you that from a selfish standpoint it would be to my advantage to preach that a person has a right to place his tithe where he wants inasmuch as on that basis additional money could be secured to undergird the responsibilities of our team. However, I know that God would not bless it. Sometime ago a dear friend of mine suggested that a group of businessmen give $10,000 a year out of their tithes to undergird this ministry God has given me. I thanked him for his generous proposal but said quite frankly, "You are barking up a tree where was never found a possum. I would no more be a party to accepting a part of a tithe of you businessmen — a tithe which is not yours, but which is God's — than I would be a party to taking a portion of your income tax — tax which is not yours, but which is Uncle Sam's."

You say, "What does this have to do with worry?" Plenty! If you went downtown and stole a hundred dollars from a merchant, would you have peace of mind? No. You would probably think that people were talking about you every time they looked at you. You would feel uncomfortable when you got in the vicinity of the business owned by the merchant whom you abused and to whom you were indebted.

In this fourth chapter of Philippians from which textual basis of our formula for victory over worry is found, Paul mentions the liberality of the Philippians. Is it not interesting that the Philippian church was the only church in which Paul found no doctrinal nor ethical error? Read the fourth chapter and notice how he commends them for their liberality in the matter of monetary stewardship. Many people glibly quote verse 19: "But my God shall supply all your need according to his riches in glory by Christ Jesus." But may I suggest that the fulfillment of that promise is conditional upon a spirit akin to that expressed by the Philippians and recorded in the immediately preceding verses?

One of the reasons that many people worry is financial adversity — an adversity sometimes begotten of their own stewardship disobedience.

> Honor the Lord with thy substance, and with the first-fruits of all thine increase:
> So shall thy barns be filled with plenty, and thy presses shall burst out with new wine.   (Proverbs 3:9,10)

He wrote those words under the inspiration of the Holy Spirit of God.

Failure to tithe is incontrovertible evidence that the guilty party is more interested in himself than he is in the work of the Lord. One of the chief causes of anxiety and worry is self-centeredness.

> Where your treasure is, there will your heart be also.
>   (Matthew 6:21)

When your chief concern is not merely how to tithe, but how to give offerings — generous offerings over and above the tithe to the glory of God — you will experience a joy and a peace the world cannot define.

When a man refuses to tithe, he does so either from ignorance or covetousness. God's Word states that covetousness is idolatry.

> Mortify therefore your members which are upon the earth; fornication, uncleanness, inordinate affection, evil concupiscence, and covetousness, which is idolatry.
>
> (Colossians 3:5)

Money becomes a tin god. Men resemble their gods; they assimilate what they conceive to be desirable. With money as your god there is no peace. But if Christ is the Lord of your life, the dominant dynamic of your experience, the overmastering passion of your interests, you inevitably begin to resemble Him who "is our peace" (Ephesians 2:14). As a result of your fellowship with Him, you begin to experience that peace that only He can give.

> Peace I leave with you, my peace I give unto you; not as the world giveth, give I unto you. Let not your heart be troubled, neither let it be afraid. (John 14:27)

Yet another word. In 1945 General MacArthur asked for ten thousand missionaries to carry the Gospel to the Orient. What an opportunity. Yet we refused to accept the challenge. Why? Simply because money was our idol and we refused to tithe our income. After all, it was going to cost as much as $2,000 per year to support a missionary. We did not send the missionaries. In 1950 there was war in Korea. We did send militarists! Instead of paying $2,000 per year, it cost us $5,000 per year — through our tax structure — to support every boy in khaki. With anxiety riding herd on us, we had the unmitigated gall to fall down on our tender knees and cry unto the Lord to spare our boys who were fighting over there, when the very warfare itself was a result of our own God-dishonoring thievery whereby we refused to pay the tithe and give offerings for the work of the Lord.

Avail yourself of the blessings (poise among them) God promises to those who honor Him with their substance.

20

Poise Through
Surrender

> Neither yield ye your members as instruments of unright-
> eousness unto sin: but yield yourselves unto God, as those
> that are alive from the dead, and your members as instru-
> ments of righteousness unto God. (Romans 6:13)

Hear the words of Paul once again:

> But what things were gain to me, those I counted loss for
> Christ.
> Yea doubtless, and I count all things but loss for the
> excellency of the knowledge of Christ Jesus my Lord: for
> whom I have suffered the loss of all things, and do count them
> but dung, that I may win Christ. (Philippians 3:7,8)

To be sure, the person who has totally surrendered himself
to Christ fulfills all the other contributory factors to poise that
have been mentioned. It may seem as though some of these
suggestions overlap, but I have put myself "on the stretch,"
as it were, to turn the diamond around and around at all angles
so that light may be flashed from every facet of it.

Certainly you have been impressed time after time when
you have listened to missionaries on furlough from a foreign
field. You have been impressed by the fact that they have
willingly forfeited economic affluence, wordly ease, the fel-

lowship of relatives and friends here at home. They have a serenity, a poise, that bespeaks a peace which cannot be defined — ''the peace of God that passeth all understanding'' (Philippians 4:7).

After hearing a returned missionary from China, a young lady walked up to her and said, ''I'd give the world to have your experience.''

''That,'' said the missionary, ''is exactly what it cost me.''

> He that findeth his life shall lose it: and he that loseth his life for my sake shall find it.   (Matthew 10:39)

Many times while in the pastorate and even on occasions since entering the field of evangelism, I have been approached by people who said, in substance, ''I know that if I yield my life to the Lord He is going to make me preach and I don't want to do it.'' With some it wasn't preaching, but some other sphere of service. There are people who apparently are plagued with the misconception that if they surrender themselves to the Lord He will require of them that which they do not want. This is a trick of the devil. When you surrender yourself to the Lord you will want what the Lord wants for you. God's Word says,

> Delight thyself also in the Lord; and he shall give thee the desires of thine heart.   (Psalm 37:4)

> If ye abide in me, and my words abide in you, ye shall ask what ye will, and it shall be done unto you.   (John 15:7)

God's Word tells us that if we, as human parents, give good gifts to our children, how much more will our Heavenly Father give good things unto them that ask Him! Now suppose that my little son would come to his mother and me and say, in substance, ''Mom and Dad, I want to do everything that will make you happy. I know that you have had much more experience than I, and there are many mistakes that I can avoid by following your counsel and advice. I beg of you to guide me and direct me. To the best of my ability I will follow your suggestions.'' Can you imagine my wife and me then going into another room and in a confidential conference saying, "Now little John Edmund has put himself completely in our hands and at our mercy. Therefore let us do everything we can to make him as awkward and miserable and frustrated as possible." That's absurd. If we would not treat our own son that way, how much more true it is that our Heavenly Father would not treat us that way.

> If ye then, being evil, know how to give good gifts unto your children, how much more shall your Father which is in heaven give good things to them that ask him?
>
> (Matthew 7:11)

> Like as a father pitieth his children, so the Lord pitieth them that fear him.   (Psalm 103:13)

With surrender comes poise that conquers worry.

Lot pitched his tent toward Sodom. Too bad. Lot was a child of God. 2 Peter 2:7,8 makes that clear. But Lot went his way instead of God's way. As a result of his disobedience he lost — lost dearly. The Lord told him to get out of Sodom. His married daughters, his sons-in-law, and his grandchildren would not leave with him. Parents may take their children to Sodom, but rarely will they ever take their children out of Sodom once they have been in Sodom for any period of time. Lot lost his wife. She was turned into a pillar of salt. He lost all his possessions, his position in the city, his prestige. He lost the respect of his two married daughters who in a cave got him drunk and then committed incest with him whereby he became the father of one son by each of his own daughters. Oh, the grief, the anxiety that would have been spared had Lot only surrendered himself to the Lord.

He was robbed of the "desires of his heart" because he refused to "delight himself in the Lord."

Some time ago, in a distant city, a mother came to me requesting an interview. She was greatly distraught mentally and emotionally. The anguish of her heart was torturing her body. She had been under psychiatric care for more than four and one-half years, during which time she had been subjected to shock treatments. She was a professing Christian and gave every evidence of sincerely wanting to do the will of God.

After some brief but pertinent probing I asked her quite frankly if there were something which had taken place in her life, whether years ago or more recently, that was constantly preying on her mind. She said there was. It was a sin committed during the days of adolescence. I asked her if she had confessed it to the Lord. She assured me that she had.

I said, "I imagine, from my observation, that you have confessed it over and over and over — probably a thousand times — to the Lord. Is that right?"

She shook her head affirmatively.

I said, "You see, actually, you are making God a liar. You confessed that sin once. God promised you absolute forgiveness as we read in the words of 1 John 1:9 — 'If we confess our sins, he is faithful and just to forgive us our sins, and to cleanse us from all unrighteousness.' "

I said, "The reason you are going through this torture is simply that you have not surrendered yourself completely to the Lord. You do not trust Him. You are not willing to take Him at His Word. He has forgiven you, but you refuse to believe it. You refuse to forgive yourself. You are making the mistake of thinking that repentance is repining and that self-examination is brooding. Now then, simply take God at His word. Surrender your life completely to Him. Surrender the limitations of your finite mind to the assurance of His immutable word. He has forgiven you. Now in complete surrender — *believe it.*"

I am happy to say there seems to be abundant evidence that the Lord has corrected the situation. She is now enjoying the poise that comes with surrender.

There are businessmen all over the nation who, petrified by fear and paralyzed by anxiety over reverses in their business, could enjoy business success and even more — the peace that passes all understanding — if they would only surrender themselves to God and take Him as their partner.

There are many homes internally divorced where husband and wife live together under protest in an atmosphere of tension simply because they refuse to surrender to Jesus Christ. It is trite, but it is nevertheless true, "If their home were built upon the Rock, Christ Jesus, it would not be headed for the rocks of chaos."

Here then is the secret of poise — surrender to Christ. Remember:

> I can do all things through Christ which strengtheneth me.
> (Philippians 4:13)

He will strengthen us to observe the laws of self-control, relaxation, scheduling, stewardship, skill, industry, thought-control, and enthusiasm — all contributory factors in the mastery of poise which brings peace and conquers worry.

Part 4

Prayer

21

Why Pray?

Paul's formula for victory over worry is Praise, Poise and Prayer. Having discussed Praise and Poise, we now come to that leg of the tripod without which the other two legs Praise and Poise cannot stand. That leg is prayer.

Be careful for nothing; but in everything by prayer and supplication with thanksgiving let your requests be made known unto God. (Philippians 4:6)

"Peace Is Possible Only to Those Who Have Related Themselves to God Through Christ — WHO IS THE PRINCE OF PEACE."

The Bible declares

There is no peace, saith my God, to the wicked.
(Isaiah 57:21)

By the wicked is not meant only the guttersnipes, ne'er-do-well's, members of the riffraff of society. By wicked is meant those who, unrepentant of their sins, have either refused or neglected to come to the Son of God by faith. They have not received Him into their hearts.

Read very carefully, for what you are about to read is a staggering truth.

> And you hath he quickened, who were dead in trespasses and sins:
>
> Wherein in time past ye walked according to the course of this world, according to the prince of the power of the air, the spirit that now worketh in the children of disobedience.
>
> (Ephesians 2:1,2)

God's Word here states that until you receive Jesus Christ as your Savior and Lord, you are ''dead in trespasses and sins.'' As one who is dead in trespasses you are dead to God and to every quality inherent in His nature.

What are these qualities? Some of them are holiness, righteousness, love, truth, wisdom, justice, power. As one who is dead to God you are therefore dead — and insensitive — to holiness, righteousness, love, truth, wisdom, justice, power. Now pause just a moment and think what that means. To be sure, those who are dead in sin and therefore dead to God have set up standards. Unfortunately they are not God's standards. ''Every man is a law unto himself.'' That explains marital discord, domestic strife, civil factiousness, labor-management antagonism, national crime and international tensions.

As one dead in sin and therefore dead to God you are alive to Satan and to the qualities inherent in his nature. Some of these qualities are sin, hostility, error, folly, injustice, weakness, fear. As a child of disobedience you are dominated and controlled by him. Read it again. He is ''the spirit that now worketh in the children of disobedience.''

Someone takes issue and says, ''Well, I'm not a drunkard. I'm not a murderer. I'm not a sex libertine. I'm not an extortionist. I'm not a troublemaker. I'm not a thief. I'm not a blasphemer.'' Of course not. It is not to Satan's interests that everyone be a drunkard, a murderer, a sex libertine, an extortionist, a troublemaker, a thief, a blasphemer.

He transforms himself as an angel of philosophic light, moral light, social-justice light, political light, cultural light.

Until you come to Jesus Christ as a self-confessed sinner and by faith accept the salvation which He has provided, you are spiritually dead. Death means separation. Physical death means separation of the body from the personality. By personality I refer to all of the unseen facets of man's being, including soul, spirit, mind and heart. Spiritual death is separation of man in this life from God. Eternal death is the irremediable and unalterable separation of the total man from God forever.

Now, because you are spiritually dead, you are separated from God. Therefore you have no peace. Nor can you have any peace. You can use the power of positive thinking, resort to Gestalt psychology, adhere to Freudian suggestions, but it all will be to no avail. Your only hope is in Christ, the Prince of Peace, through whom you have access to God.

Life is union just as death is separation. Physical life is the union of the body and the personality. Spiritual life is the union of man in this life with God through Christ. Eternal life is synonymous with spiritual life.

When you receive the Lord Jesus Christ as your Savior you do not receive simply a new concept or a new creed, or a new formula for living. You receive a Person. It is "Christ in you" (Colossians 1:27). You receive a new nature.

> Whereby are given unto us exceeding great and precious promises: that by these ye might be *partakers of the divine nature,* having escaped the corruption that is in the world through lust. (2 Peter 1:4)

Eternal life is the life of God in the soul of the believer. So that, for the child of God, that which we call physical death is but a transition from life to life more abundant, from time to eternity, from the finite into the infinite. Therefore when one receives spiritual life he receives in kind, though not in degree, right here and now, everything that he will enjoy in heaven: communion with God, the favor of God, victory over sin, a transcendent love, divine motivation and *peace*.

As mentioned, the formula for peace — victory over worry — is Praise, Poise, and Prayer. No unbeliever can have this perfect peace, for unbelievers cannot pray. God will not hear them. Unbelievers do not have the privilege of prayer.

The prayer of the unrighteous is an abomination before God (Proverbs 28:9).

God will not hear those who persist in unbelief.

> If I regard iniquity in my heart, the Lord will not hear me.
> (Psalm 66:18)

The only way anyone can come to God is through Jesus Christ.

> Jesus saith unto him, I am the way, the truth, and the life:
> no man cometh unto the Father, but by me.   (John 14:6)

The blind man whom Christ healed in John 9 stated the truth — a truth that is refuted nowhere in God's Word — when he said:

> Now we know that God heareth not sinners; but if any man
> be a worshipper of God, and doeth his will, him he heareth.
> (John 9:31)

Prayer is a family matter — a matter between God the Father, and born-again believers, His children.

Worry is a weakness of the flesh. You cannot conquer a weakness of the flesh in the energy of the flesh. It must be done in the power of God. Prayer gives you access to that power.

Prayer is fundamental because it makes available to you the divine dynamic whereby you master the mechanics leading to victory over worry. Prayer is essential to Praise. Prayer is essential to Poise. God shows us what we must do for victory. In response to prayer He channels to us through the indwelling Holy Spirit the ability to do what we ought to do — obey His commandments.

Prayer raises us to God's level. It takes us into God's atmosphere. It brings us into communion and intimacy with God.

Prayer signifies dependence upon God. Without Him we can do nothing. With Him we can do everything. He is the source of our strength.

> I can do all things through Christ which strengtheneth me.
> (Philippians 4:13)

He is the source of our resources.

> But my God shall supply all your need according to his riches in glory by Christ Jesus. (Philippians 4:19)

The Grecian says, "Man, know thyself." The Roman says, "Man, rule thyself." The Chinese says, "Man, improve thyself." The Buddhist says, "Man, annihilate thyself." The Brahman says, "Man, submerge thyself in the universal sum of all." The Moslem says, "Man, submit thyself." The twentieth-century internationalist says, "Man, learn the art and practice the principles of peaceful coexistence." But Christ says, *"Without me you can do nothing"* (John 15:5).

Conversely, with Him we can do anything.

Prayer is the means whereby we make contact with God's strength and in Him overcome our weakness.

Only when we set aside our own strength will the Lord really become our strength.

Attempt to float. As long as you exercise your own efforts to keep up you will go down. Give yourself up to the water and it will immediately sweep under you with its waves and bear you up in its strength.

The Lord Himself is our strength. Don't pray, "Lord, give me strength," as though you are asking Him for a quality distinct from Himself. Rather say, "O Lord, be Thou my strength."

Listen to Ephesians 3:20:

> Now unto him that is able to do exceeding abundantly above all that we ask or think, according to *the power that worketh in us.*

Here again you have that word *energeo.* And the word translated power is the word *dunamis* from which we get the word *dynamic.* Just as Satan and his "powers of darkness" energize the unbeliever, so God energizes the obedient Christian. He becomes the divine dynamic whereby the believer conquers all things — including worry.

The same power that burnishes each star, points each blade of grass, hurls each wave upon the shore, formed the body of our Savior, raised Jesus from the dead, and will raise our bodies or transfigure them in the hour of glory, is the same power which is available to each obedient Christian. This power is made available through prayer.

This power is available only to those who are weak. God's helpfulness is meted out only to those who confess their helplessness.

> And he said unto me, My grace is sufficient for thee: for my strength is made perfect in weakness. Most gladly therefore will I rather glory in my infirmities, that the power of Christ may rest upon me.
>
> Therefore I take pleasure in infirmities, in reproaches, in necessities, in persecutions, in distresses for Christ's sake: for when I am weak, then am I strong.
>
> (2 Corinthians 12:9,10)

Our strength lies in childlike helplessness. In your helplessness through prayer, cast yourself upon Him who is our strength. The very essence of the meaning of prayer is that you need help beyond your own strength.

The reason many of us do not pray is that we are too strong — strong in our own false, swaggering, blustering strength. We are strong in our own strength, the very heart of which is utter helplessness, emptiness, and weakness.

Worry is an intrusion into God's province. You are making yourself the father of the household instead of the child. You are setting yourself up as the master of God's Kingdom, instead of the servant for whom the Master provides.

The basis of prayer is man's need and God's ability to meet that need. When one really prays he is confessing his utter helplessness. He is casting himself completely and wholly upon God. He is delighting himself in the Lord. Consequently the Lord grants unto him the desires of his heart.

Our needs are manifold. Our perplexities are multifarious and variegated. Don't worry. Instead, turn your care into a prayer. Follow the example of Paul who said, "I conferred not with flesh and blood" (Galatians 1:16). Conferring with flesh and blood about your worries instead of taking them to God is a fruitful cause for increased worry.

Years ago, while I was still in the pastorate, I concluded a Sunday night service with the benediction. Even before the choir's response had ended, an anxious woman rushed up to me and asked if I would talk with her child who was under conviction of sin and wanted to be saved.

It was my joy to see that keen and energetic youngster enter into peace with God through Christ. We had prayer together. As I rose to dismiss them, I realized that the mother was in agony, and she looked at me as if to say, "I am in such trouble. Can you help me?"

I asked her if she would like to speak with me. She grabbed the opportunity as a drowning man would grab a life belt. I asked the youngster to step into the next office for just a moment. Turning to the mother I said, "All right. Would you like to share with me the problem that is causing you this grief?" She burst into uncontrollable sobs. I assured her that having been pastor of a church of over three thousand members for several years I was now shockproof. I further reminded her that everything would be in strictest confidence.

Let me stop here long enough to tell you that this lady was one of the outstanding members of the church. She taught a Sunday school class, was prominent in the Training Union and in the Women's Missionary Society. She almost never missed a service. She tithed her money. She knew her Bible. If Gallup had taken a poll of the membership, I am sure this lady would have ranked among the most respected of all members.

Finally, she blurted out her story. I sat transfixed with astonishment as she told the most sordid story of duplicity and sin I ever had heard from a supposedly respectable woman.

Finally she nearly screamed out, "Preacher, have I committed the unpardonable sin?" It was my joy to assure her from God's Word that if she still desired to repent, God would receive her. I assured her in the words of Jesus who said, ". . . him that cometh to me I will in no wise cast out" (John 6:37b).

For eleven years she had been trying to win in her own

strength the battle of life. Though not yet forty she had already aged considerably. Her health was poor. She was under psychiatric care. Finally she came to Christ.

Today she is a charming, radiant Christian. Her health is fine. Her mind is free from personality-corroding, body-debilitating, mind-destroying worry.

It wasn't until she confessed her helplessness and cast herself wholly upon God that she received strength to live dynamically. Now, as a child of God, she has a prayer life by which she maintains communion with God and keeps un-clogged the channel through which His strength is released to her moment by moment and day by day.

Pray because prayer is essential to poise. Recall the story of Daniel in the lions' den. You remember that he had been hounded by the men who were bent upon his destruction. Nevertheless, he did not alter his habit one iota. There was no ruffling of his spirit. He continued to make his prayer unto God three times a day. He prayed in a spirit of deep humility, recognizing his absolute dependence upon God. Was this a sign of weakness? No! It was a sign of strength. To be sure, Daniel put his face in the dust before God, but he did not lose his courage before the wrath of Darius. He sobbed like a heartbroken child when he knelt before his God, but he faced without a quiver the jaws of the hungry lions. What poise!

There is a real efficiency in prayer. This fact ought also to induce a greater interest in prayer. Martin Luther was not talking through his hat when he said, "I have so much business I cannot get along without spending three hours daily in prayer." Prayer is efficient in that it saves time. It saves time by conditioning you for the day's activities and personal contacts. It saves time by conditioning those with whom you will associate. It saves time in that it makes available to you wisdom which in turn leads to quick and proper decisions.

> If any of you lack wisdom, let him ask of God, that giveth to all men liberally, and upbraideth not; and it shall be given him.   (James 1:5)

This of course leads to peace of mind. How many people

there are who fret and mope around wasting precious time simply because they don't know what to do or how to do what they need to do. The Lord has promised them the needed wisdom, but they either refuse it or neglect to avail themselves of it. The resultant loss of peace and time is incalculable.

Let me digress here for just a moment. In Chapter 23 stress is given to the importance of definite periods of prayer and waiting upon the Lord in prayer. You have just read the words of James 1:5. How ridiculous it is for the Christian to ask for wisdom and immediately terminate his prayer taking leave of Him who is the Source of wisdom before He has had time to impart it. What would you think of a man who walked into your home and with apparent earnestness asked you a question, but turned around and walked out before you had time to answer it? Remember, prayer is not a one-way street. It is a two-way street.

Prayer is efficient because it puts you in touch with *infinite intelligence*. Prayer will dispel the fogs of human ignorance. It banishes the darkness of self-destructive errors in judgment. People of prayer, regardless of their academic limitations, are the recipients of a proper perspective and a keen understanding imparted to them by Him who is "the Truth."

Prayer is efficient in that it makes available to you the grace necessary to black out negative thoughts, distracting attitudes, and worries which torture the mind and deteriorate the body. Through prayer we cast

> . . . down imaginations, and every high thing that exalteth itself against the knowledge of God, and bringing into captivity every thought to the obedience of Christ.
>
> (2 Corinthians 10:5)

When your thoughts are Christ's, they are not worry thoughts.

Prayer is efficient in that it enlists divine strength enabling you to effect the proper execution of your God-given responsibilities. While in the flesh upon this earth our Lord prayed before every great endeavor.

Prayer is efficient in that it can lead to the correction of circumstances that both consume time and saddle a person with destructive grief. Do you remember the prayer of Moses and Aaron on behalf of their sister Miriam who was suffering with leprosy? How would that story have ended had it not been for their prayer?

Prayer is efficient in that it leads to harmony. Read once again the first chapters of the Acts of the Apostles. How differently history would have been written had it not been for the prayer of the 120 in the upper room. The harmony that prevailed between them was one of the by-products of their prayer lives. We read concerning them, "and all that believed were together, and had all things common" (Acts 2:3, 4). Worry cannot survive in an atmosphere of such harmony.

Prayer is efficient because it is productive of faith. And faith, of course, is the antidote to worry. Faith is acting in confidence upon the word of another. The one who is faithful in his prayer life acts in confidence upon God's Word. He goes to God with all his dilemmas, all of his assets and all of his liabilities. He acts in confidence upon God's Word which tells him that if he delights himself in the Lord, the Lord will give him the desires of his heart. He prays. God answers his prayer. The very answer is productive of greater faith — of a more eager and a more earnest disposition to act in confidence upon God's Word.

Prayer is efficient because it leads to inner security. The person who spends time regularly in prayer comes to know in his inmost soul that God's Word is true when He assures us, ". . . I will never leave thee, nor forsake thee" (Hebrews 13:5). The resulting inner assurance leads to much greater efficiency. For instance, I know a man who is going broke simply because he insists on picking up the tab at the restaurant every time he and his friends are eating out. If he goes to the ball game with ten or fifteen other folks he insists on paying the bill. He is constantly giving away expensive gifts — gifts he simply cannot afford. Why? His dreadful insecurity is the only answer I can conceive. He is compensating for the lack of inner security in his mad effort to secure the fervent friendship of a host of people whose gracious responses to his generosity give him a temporary sense of well-being.

When a man is properly related to God he has within himself all of the ingredients necessary to provide him with security, joy and peace regardless of external conditions. This relationship is only maintained as man spends time regularly with God.

Why pray? Pray because prayer is the means whereby you permit, yea, invite God to so energize you that to His glory you live victoriously, overcoming the world, the flesh and the devil.

Yes, pray because through prayer you enlist the power of the Spirit of God to conquer the weakness of the flesh — *even worry*. When your thoughts are Christ's, they are not worry thoughts.

Pray, because through prayer you have opportunity to turn every care into a prayer.

22

How to Pray

Once again,

> Be careful for nothing; but in every thing by prayer and supplication with thanksgiving let your requests be made known unto God.
> (Philippians 4:6)

In this verse, three different Greek words for prayer are introduced. The first word, translated "prayer," refers to a general offering up of wishes and desires to God. This word points to the frame of mind required in the petitioner — a mind of devotion. The word refers to unrestricted concourse between man and God. That which brings greatest glory to God and profit to you is the habit of prayer. We might call it the Prayer Mood or the Prayer Disposition.

The word translated "supplication" comes from a Greek word meaning "entreaty," a "seeking," "need," "indigence." It refers to an entreaty impelled by a great sense of need, an extreme want. In fact, the verb form of this word in the original means "to want." Therefore this word refers distinctly to the petitionary prayers that are expressive of personal need. This prayer is a special petition for the supply of wants, an act of solicitation.

The third word used and translated in the King James,

"requests," refers to requests and even more strongly to demands.

Now the word translated in the King James, "prayer," includes adoration, thanksgiving, confession and intercession.

The word translated "supplication" refers strictly to an entreaty to God to supply our needs and our wants. On the basis of the teaching of Philippians 4:6 it would be well for us to ponder several factors involved in effectual praying.

If you would have victory over worry, pray *intelligently*. "Let your requests be made known unto God." I heard of a certain man who spent six hours in prayer each day. Lest he should go to sleep when on board a boat, he stood upright and had a rope stretched across, so that he might lie against it. If he slept he would fall. His object was to keep on for six hours with what he called prayer. What sort of prayer was it? He kept on repeating, "There is no God, but God. There is no God, but God." He repeated the same thing over and over again. He did not plead with God to give him anything. Just as a witch repeats a charm, so he repeated certain words. That is not praying.

If you go on your knees and simply repeat a certain formula, you are speaking only words. You are not praying. Some people are criticized for using beads and fetishes to "say prayers." But there are many Protestants who just as definitely "say prayers." They do not pray. They repeat formulas. They say prayers as did the farmer who each night prayed, "O Lord, bless me, my wife, my son John, his wife, us four, no more. Amen." God does not hear you for your much speaking.

Even though on Mount Carmel the wild-eyed multitude cut themselves and chanted repetitiously, "O Baal, hear us!" they were not praying. Let your *requests* be made known unto God.

Get alone with God and tell Him what you want. Pour out your heart before Him. He does not care for high-flown language. Study the prayers of the Bible and you will be impressed that there was no formal phraseology, and there was no fixed and mechanical use of words. Go to God as you go to your mother, your father, your friend.

Don't think that simply because you get on your knees for a spell every morning and every night God is going to dissipate your worries. Pray intelligently. Tell Him your problem. Tell Him that you have sinned — that you have worried. Tell Him that you want victory over it. Be specific.

And that leads me to say if you would have victory over worry, pray *definitely*. In Chapters 1 and 3 you learned what worry does to you physically. You also learned that worry is a sin. Therefore, as a worrier, you have a great need. Offer up supplications to the Lord — ''entreaties expressive of your personal need that solicit God's answer for that need.''

Indefinite praying is usually halfhearted praying. Indefinite praying is often insincere praying. It is usually a mere formality. There is no burden, no urgency, no overwhelming constraint in indefinite praying. Indefinite praying shows that one is not sure of the will of God. Therefore he knows not what to pray for. It often indicates that one is trusting in the *act* of praying rather than in the God who answers prayer.

The mind of man is so constituted that it cannot fasten its desires *intensely* upon numerous things at the same time. Jesus said,

> Therefore I say unto you, What things soever ye desire, when ye pray, believe that ye receive them, and ye shall have them.
> (Mark 11:24)

Now it is impossible to desire strongly that which is not definite.

Your problem is worry. Pray definitely about this problem. Pray definitely that God will give you victory over your distrust of Him. Pray that God will forgive you for intruding into His own province by trying to carry on His business. Ask Him for the grace to cast all your cares upon Him.

In addition to all this, pray specifically concerning the problems causing your anxiety. If it is a wayward daughter, pray definitely and specifically for God's will to be done in her life and for God to give you the grace in the meantime to live triumphantly.

If it is financial difficulty, pray definitely that God will show you if you have been unwise in the handling of your money. If you have been unwise, ask Him to forgive you. Pray definitely that He will give you wisdom and grace to do what you can. Pray that He will miraculously do what you can't do. Then rest in the truth of Psalm 37:25, "I have been young, and now am old; yet have I not seen the righteous forsaken, nor his seed begging bread."

If you are suffering from a nervous stomach pray definitely about it. Don't simply say, "Lord, take away my nervous stomach." Find out what are the causes of your condition. Be specific. Be definite. And then let your request be made known unto God. Or, as we could correctly translate it, "make known your demands."

Every now and then I hear people say, "God heard my prayer, but He answered it a little differently than I was expecting." That is ridiculous. What would you think of me if I had five sons and I prayed, "Lord, save my five sons." A few days later my neighbor's five sons all went to church and professed faith in Jesus Christ. Supposing that I said, "Praise God; He answered my prayer. I prayed for the salvation of my five sons and He answered my prayer. He saved the five sons of my next door neighbor." That is nonsense.

Pray definitely and expect a definite answer. Pray for bread. God will give you bread, not a stone. Pray for fish. God will give you a fish, not a serpent.

If you would have victory over worry, pray *importunately*. The word *importunate* means both "demandingly" and "persistently." These qualities are consistent with the text. Remember, the words *requests* can be translated "demands." The tense used is the present imperative so that we might translate the words this way — "in everything by general concourse with God and specific entreaties arising out of personal needs, with thanksgiving, let your demands be made known *perpetually* unto God."

You can make these demands because of your relationship with God through Christ. "But my God shall supply all your

need according to his riches in glory by Christ Jesus''
(Philippians 4:19).

He has promised to supply all your needs. You can demand
the fulfillment of that promise with this warning, however.
You are not to say, ''Lord, supply all of my needs.'' Rather
you are to specifically and definitely make known those needs
one by one. And then pray persistently. Your cares are
persistent. Therefore make your prayers persistent.

Pray to God and then pray again. If the Lord does not
answer you the first time, be grateful that you have good
reason for praying again. If He does not answer your requests
the second time, thank Him that He loves you so much that He
wants to hear your voice again. If He keeps you waiting
until you have gone to Him seven times, say to yourself,
''Now I know that I worship the God of Elijah, for Elijah's
God let him go again seven times before the blessing was
given.''

Count it an honor to be permitted to wrestle in prayer even
as Jacob wrestled with the angel during the long watches of
the night. This is the way God develops His princes.

Jacob never would have been ISRAEL— Prince with God—
if he had received the blessing from the angel at the first
asking. He kept on wrestling until he prevailed. Then he
became a prince of God. Worry cannot exist with this kind of
prayer.

Jesus taught us to pray all the way through the gospels.
Two great illustrations He gave to us in the eleventh and in
the eighteenth chapters of Luke.

The man who wanted to borrow bread at midnight is a
striking example of the spirit Jesus desires to inculcate. The
borrower was in dire need. He was terribly in earnest and
would not take no for an answer. Jesus said when you pray be
just as earnest and be just as persistent as this man was. You
need the blessing of God much more than he needed his three
loaves. You are seeking something that means more than
bread, and just as the importunity of the borrower finally wins
out, so the soul set upon finding God will command His
attention and be heard.

God has no time for lukewarm pleas, for easygoing, halfhearted prayers. If the sense of need is not great, if you forget about the matter before the day is over, God will pay little heed to your prayer. If you have something vital at issue, if you are willing to give time and effort, and if you press your claim home to a finish, God will listen. The man who is willing to quit, or who can quit, is not in the condition of mind and heart to appreciate the favor of God. The soul who counts it the biggest privilege on earth to know God, who seeks for Him and His blessings as men seek for silver and gold, will not only be rewarded, but also will be conditioned to estimate rightly what has been received.

Jesus then adds:

> And I say unto you, Ask, and it shall be given you; seek, and ye shall find; knock, and it shall be opened unto you.
> For every one that asketh receiveth; and he that seeketh findeth; and to him that knocketh it shall be opened.
>
> (Luke 11:9,10)

This is not the easy passage some people think it is. It does not mean that all you have to do is ask for something and receive it, or to knock and the door flies open. It refers to a life which is one continual search after God, a constant seeking, a daily asking, a habitual knocking.

This is the only antidote to worry which itself is perpetual. Let your prayer be perpetual. It means that you must desire that which lies behind the closed door intensely enough to knock with unshaken persistence. Jesus is here saying that to such knocking the door will open. To seeking of that sort will come the answer which makes life full and rich.

The parable found in the eighteenth chapter of Luke is still more striking, as it represents a case where the delayed answer is misunderstood. The petitioner is set forth in the figure of a poor widow seeking vindication and protection from an unjust judge. The judge is the perfect embodiment of heartless wickedness. No more complete portrait of utter depravity was ever drawn than Jesus sketched in that one terse sentence, "which feared not God, neither regarded man" (Luke 18:2). Just one stroke of the Master Artist's brush, and the cold, heartless man stands before us; one who regards not suffering humanity nor fears the coming judgment of God.

The feeble, insignificant petitioner was scorned. No heed was given, but Jesus said she continued to press her plea for justice until in absolute selfishness and for no other reasons the judge granted the request.

> . . . Though I fear not God, nor regard man; Yet because this widow troubleth me, I will avenge her, lest by her continual coming she weary me.   (Luke 18:4b,5)

The argument is: If a man like that can be moved to do what means nothing to him, will not God hear the continual cry of His people He loves with a boundless compassion? There are long periods when prayers seem unanswered. There are long days of darkness, sometimes years of wearisome waiting, while countless petitions are sent to a heaven that seems deaf and empty. This is the time about which Jesus speaks. He says, "Cry on, God will hear. He is not heartless, neither has He forgotten."

This parable is for the time when faith has staggered and the heart has grown sick with waiting. Let us remember that the longest delay to us may be as the twinkling of an eye to the plans of God. Alexander Maclaren said years ago, "Heaven's clock does not beat in the same note with our little chronometers." Jesus teaches us to pray on. He says we must not quit. We must not doubt. God knows when to answer. He knows the best time and the most fitting place. We can, in all confidence, leave the question of *when* and *where* to Him. Of one thing we may be sure — *He will answer*. Worthy prayer does not become discouraged. It does not surrender. This is the power that defeats worry.

If you would conquer worry, *pray in faith*. Faith is acting in confidence upon the word of another. Faith in God is acting in confidence upon His Word. You were saved that way. It is also in this way you become mighty with God.

You develop faith as you meditate upon God's Word — the Bible.

> So then faith cometh by hearing, and hearing by the word
> of God. (Romans 10:17)

Prayer and the Word of God are inseparably connected. "Feasting" on the Word of God is productive of that faith without which prayer is useless.

Through the Word of God the Lord speaks to our hearts and conditions our hearts for prayer. In prayer we speak to Him in faith. So many times in the Scriptures we have passages indicating that the Lord spoke first, after which the one who heard the Word of the Lord spoke to Him in prayer. Read Jeremiah 1:4-6 as an example.

> Then the word of the Lord came unto me, saying,
> Before I formed thee in the belly I knew thee; and before thou camest forth out of the womb I sanctified thee, and I ordained thee a prophet unto the nations.
> Then said I, Ah, Lord God! behold, I cannot speak: for I am a child.

You remember also Daniel's great prayer. In the first year of the reign of King Darius we see Daniel reading the Word of God. He had in his hand the prophecy of Jeremiah in which the Lord had promised that the desolation of Jerusalem should last seventy years. After reading this prophetic promise Daniel turned to the Lord. The reading of the Word of God led to prayer. The reading of God's Word was productive of the faith that made prayer effectual.

The German theologian Bengel had the reputation of being a great man of prayer, one who knew the secret of effectual prayer. One day a fellow believer watched him at the close of the day. He saw the old saint sitting before a large Bible, reading slowly, often stopping, meditating with the silent tears running down his cheeks. After reading and meditating a long time, Bengel closed the Book and began to speak to God in prayer. His heart had been prepared through the reading of the Word. Neglect of the daily reading of the Word of God and meditation on it soon results in neglected prayer as well.

The secret to earnest and effectual prayer — the prayer of

faith — is faithful and diligent study of the Scriptures.

Faith is essential to effectual prayer. All real prayer has as its basis a firm faith in a God who responds to the quest of the human soul.

> But without faith it is impossible to please him: for he that cometh to God must believe that he is, and that he is a rewarder of them that diligently seek him. (Hebrews 11:6)

We come to God by our hearts and not by our intellects. The first condition of entering into His fellowship is a faith, not only that God is, but that He will be found by the soul who honestly and persistently seeks for Him. God is not found by those who look for Him in the spirit of cold curiosity. He is not found by those who simply desire to extend the range of their intellectual conquest. This is the reason why many self-styled philosophers and many pseudoscientists have been unable to come to any clear conception of God. It was to men of this type that Zophar said,

> Canst thou by searching find out God? canst thou find out the Almighty unto perfection? (Job 11:7)

When a man says in the pride of his intellect, "I will now see if there be any God," he may turn his telescope upon the farthest heavens and count the myriad worlds that wander in the blue abyss. He may peer among the atoms and divide and subdivide the electrons, but the greatest thing in the universe will still be hidden from his eyes.

The laws of logic, the theories of philosophy, the investigation of chemistry and physics, all have their place and are of great value, but they are not milestones on the road into fellowship with God. The man who can say with the Hebrew psalmist, "My soul thirsteth for God, for the living God: when shall I come and appear before God?" (Psalm 42:2), is more nearly on the road to His presence. The humble man who with simple and sincere faith reaches out after God will find Him while the philosopher is groping in the shadows of his theories and the scientist is bewildered with the problems of his laboratory.

If you would enter into the prayer life that conquers care

life, spend some time each day with the Word of God. The time spent will be productive of faith that pleases God. This time spent will condition you for communion with God and as you commune with God you will develop ever more confidence in God and this glorious cycle will continue unabated as long as life shall last.

You worry. Here is God's Word that if you will utilize this formula of praise, poise and prayer He will give you peace. He also makes it clear that by prayer you will be given strength to offer praise and to manifest poise. As you pray you will become effective in prayer. Now believe this. Believe that He will give you precisely what He has promised to give you if you will meet the conditions. He will give you *peace*.

He cannot go back upon His promise. He is "the God, that cannot lie" (Titus 1:2).

Some of you pray, but you only say words. While you are asking God to give you victory over worry, you are at the very time worrying that you are not praying correctly. You are worrying that maybe you have not met all of the conditions. *Stop psychoanalyzing yourself.* Don't be a spiritual hypochondriac. *Get your mind off yourself and on to God. Spend enough time in your prayer thanking Him for what He has done and praising Him for who He is that you will be conditioned to pray intelligently, definitely, importunately, and in faith.*

As you pray, picture yourself a perfectly adjusted, dynamic, radiant personality living in the strength of God to the glory of God. This is certainly God's will for you. By faith, then, take God at His Word, lay hold upon Him in prayer and become the personality to glorify Him and bring peace to your mind. You are what you think you are. Stop, therefore, insulting God. Recognize yourself as a redeemed soul. You are a child of the King. You are in league with the Creative Power of the universe. Recognize yourself as a potential recipient of qualities, attitudes, and resources that will glorify God and bless your fellowman as you live triumphantly over every worry and care.

If you would conquer worry, pray *privately*.

> But thou, when thou prayest, enter into thy closet, and
> when thou hast shut thy door, pray to thy Father which is in
> secret; and thy Father which seeth in secret shall reward thee
> openly.   (Matthew 6:6)

God deals with men face to face and heart to heart. You
cannot have audience with a king and be engaged with the
crowd at the same time. The matters between you and God
are too sacred and personal to be laid bare to the eyes of the
crowd. Furthermore, prayer calls for such concentration,
such focalization, such rallying of all of our powers, that it
demands the quiet of the inner chamber. We are going to
share with God when we pray things which we would not for
the very life of us share with the crowd. There are the secrets
of our hearts to be talked over with Him. There are sins that
need to be confessed to Him. There are yearnings and hunger-
ings of our deepest souls to whisper into His ear about which
we would not for anything speak to our dearest friend. Then
God wants a real opportunity to speak to us. "The still, small
voice" cannot be heard amidst jarring sounds, shattering
voices, the hum of machinery, or the clamor of business.

Jesus did not mean that no man could pray unless in an
empty and quiet room. He did mean that the door of mind and
heart would shut out the world. The outside world must be
locked away from the private transactions which take place
there. "When thou hast shut thy door," when there is no one
there but God and you, when you are all alone with Him, then
pray.

It is so true that when we really pray, no one is there but
God and ourselves. All else is outside. When we pray, our
dearest earthly friend is outside the door. He may be in the
same pew, in the same room, but he is outside the door.
Every business affair is without. Every allurement of the
world is without. All the silver that shines and the jewels that
sparkle are outside the locked door when we really pray. Not
a distraction, not an alien sound! How quiet it must be in
there! One can almost hear the beating of his heart and the

rustle of his thoughts. That door is not made of steel or lumber. It is the door of our will that closes and says to all the world, "Out. Out. Out. I have great business at hand! I am engaged with the Almighty. Keep out!"

I tell you, worry cannot abide when you are locked up with God in the secret sanctuary of prayer.

If you would conquer worry, pray *thankfully*. This will lead your mind to revert back to Chapter 6. The text says that we are to pray and supplicate "with thanksgiving." The kind of prayer that kills worry is a prayer that asks cheerfully, joyfully, thankfully.

Pray, "Lord, I am in financial straits. I bless Thee for this condition and I ask Thee to supply all my needs." This is the way to pray. "Lord, I am sick. I thank Thee for this affliction for Thou hast promised that 'all things work together for good to them that love the Lord.' Now heal me, I beseech Thee — if it please Thee!" Or you will pray, "Lord, I am in great trouble. I thank Thee for this trouble for I know that it contains a blessing even though the envelope is black-edged. Now, Lord, give me grace as I pass through this trouble." This kind of prayer kills worry.

If you would conquer worry, pray in *Jesus' name*.

> If ye shall ask any thing in my name, I will do it.
>
> (John 14:14)
>
> And in that day ye shall ask me nothing. Verily, verily, I say unto you, Whatsoever ye shall ask the Father in my name, he will give it you.
>
> Hitherto have ye asked nothing in my name: ask, and ye shall receive, that your joy may be full.
>
> These things have I spoken unto you in proverbs: but the time cometh, when I shall no more speak unto you in proverbs, but I shall shew you plainly of the Father.
>
> At that day ye shall ask in my name: and I say not unto you, that I will pray the Father for you:
>
> For the Father himself loveth you, because ye have loved me, and have believed that I came out from God.
>
> (John 16:23-27)

Years ago I was involved in a four-car accident. Litigation

proceedings began almost immediately. I needed help desperately. I needed the resources of the greatest accident lawyer in the country. His name was Weinstein. His fee was understandably large. So large that I, as a ministerial student, could not meet its demands. However, a dear friend of mine hearing of my need, came to see me. This friend was part owner of a large company in Chicago. He said, "Haggai, Weinstein is our lawyer. We retain him. Here, let me give you one of my cards." On the back of the card he scribbled a note of introduction to Weinstein. Weinstein saw me. He solved my legal problem. Why? Because of a fee I paid? Not at all. Because of the fee paid by my friend. He received me in the name of and on the merits of my friend.

The Lord Jesus Christ is my Friend "that sticketh closer than a brother." He paid the fee that I could not pay — the penalty of sin. He paid it with His own blood. In His name and on His merits I have access to God who alone can solve my problems.

Catch this insight. Grasp this concept. And you will be well on the way to the conquest of worry.

23

When to Pray

The tense used in Philippians 4:6 is present imperative. It carries the idea of durative action. Therefore we are being true to the meaning of the text when we translate Philippians 4:6, "Don't worry about anything whatever, but in all things by prayer and supplication with thanksgiving, let your requests be made known *perpetually* to God."

The present imperative tense is also used in the first part of the verse. In other words, Paul is saying, "Don't perpetually worry, but *perpetually* pray." *Let perpetual prayer take the place of perpetual care*.

Prayer is the Christian's breath. When breathing is obstructed, health is jeopardized. When the Christian permits any obstruction to his prayer life, his spiritual health is put in jeopardy.

Our little son breathed only once every two and a half minutes the first three hours he was in this world. Because of his deficient breathing only an inadequate supply of oxygen could reach the brain with the result that brain tissues were destroyed and body movement was impaired. Many Christians are suffering from spiritual cerebral palsy. An inadequate supply of the oxygen of prayer has destroyed spiritual fiber and impaired Christian effectiveness.

Breath is essential to life and health. The breath of prayer is essential to Christian well-being. When the Christian is praying, he is breathing spiritually. Just as we must breathe ceaselessly, so we must pray ceaselessly.

The injunction of God's Word is that we "Pray without ceasing" (1 Thessalonians 5:17).

The trouble with many of us is that we pray when caught in the swirl of difficulty, oppression and vicious circumstances. Then we think of Psalm 50:15:

> . . . call upon me in the day of trouble: I will deliver thee, and thou shalt glorify me.

The story is told of two Irishmen, Pat and Mike, who had narrowly escaped death on a sinking ship. They were floundering around in icy ocean waters on a couple of planks. Pat was addicted to the grossest profanity but he decided to repent of it if the Lord would come to his rescue. Mike thought his theology sound. Pat assumed the countenance of a horrified Mohammedan at Mecca and began to pray. Just before arriving at the main thesis of his repentant prayer, Mike spotted a ship coming toward them. As delighted as Columbus when he first spotted the North American shore, Mike hollered, "Hold it, Pat. Don't commit yerself. Here's a ship." Pat immediately stopped praying! Isn't that the way many of us are? The only time we pray is when we are in a jam. As soon as things improve we forget God.

Spiritually speaking, most of us can much better afford adversity than prosperity. Like the Israelites of old, it seems that when our prosperity expands, our spirituality contracts. Like Mike, we call upon the Lord as long as things are precarious, but as soon as things improve we resort to our own resources. The Lord is but an escape mechanism for some.

The Christian's prayer life is one of incessant prayer. "Praying always," says Paul in Ephesians 6:18. That is, praying at all seasons and on all occasions. If you would conquer worry, you must always maintain a spirit of prayer. You must live in a prayerful disposition.

"Pray without ceasing." One of my theological professors, in discussing the meaning of 1 Thessalonians 5:17, told of an experience of some ministers. They had congregated early and were waiting for the Monday morning ministers' meeting. They were talking in the vestibule and this verse was mentioned. Discussion became spirited and the meaning of this verse evoked no small comment — and consternation. It wasn't long until they readily agreed that the verse puzzled them. How could one possibly pray without ceasing? A scrub woman about her work overheard them and said, "Excuse me, gentlemen. But it's all very simple." She then gave her interpretation of the verse in the form of a personal illustration.

She said, "I always pray. When I go to bed at night I thank the Lord for the joy of resting on His everlasting arms. When I awaken the next morning I ask Him to open my eyes that I may behold new and wondrous things out of His Word. When I bathe I ask Him to cleanse me from secret faults. When I dress I ask Him to clothe me with humility and love. When building the fire I ask Him to build the fire of love for souls in my heart. When I eat I ask Him to cause me to grow on the bread of His Word." On and on she continued explaining to those ministers the way in which she lived in the attitude of prayer. Prayer was her habit. They marveled. They grasped the truth. We are to "pray without ceasing."

In praying without ceasing one's mind is stayed on Christ. One is constantly attuned to the will of God. While one may not be involved in deliberate and conscious contact with Him, one is nevertheless aware of His presence and one's life is regulated by His will. It is much the same as a mother who goes to sleep at night. The little baby is in the crib. The mother is sleeping. Even while sleeping, however, she is attuned to the baby's needs and wants. The slightest whimper of the baby arouses her from sleep. So in the life of the Christian who prays without ceasing. He is attuned to the will of God. God's slightest suggestion, command or desire arouses the believer to obedience and action.

In Isaiah we read: "Thou wilt keep him in perfect peace,

whose mind is stayed on thee: because he trusteth in thee"
(Isaiah 26:3). When you pray without ceasing, you are "attuned" to God. When you live in an awareness of His will,
your mind is "stayed" on Him. Now the truth is simply this.
When your mind is stayed on Him, you have perfect peace.
When you have perfect peace you don't have worry. If you
would conquer worry, it is essential that you live in the
atmosphere of prayer.

The pages of God's Word are replete with the names of
those who prayed. All who had power with God and men
were people of prayer. Explain the poise of Daniel in the
lions' den apart from the mighty prayer life he maintained.

Moses prayed until his face glistened with the glory of
God.

The great example, of course, is our Lord. His whole life
was a prayer. Before He did anything He prayed. After He
did anything He prayed. He prayed morning, noon and night.
Sometimes He prayed all night. Whenever He was alone He
prayed. Prayer was never off His lips and was never out of
His heart. He was the incarnation of this truth, "Pray without
ceasing."

Let me caution you against a prevalent mistake. There are
those who say, "I always pray. When I am driving the car
down the street I pray. When I go about my business I pray. I
never spend great periods of time alone with God in prayer. I
simply pray all the time in whatever I do." This is well and
good. But it is also essential that one set apart a period each
day when he can get alone with God and pray.

Charles Simeon devoted four hours each morning to
prayer. Mr. Wesley spent two hours daily in prayer. It is said
that John Fletcher stained the walls with the breath of his
prayers. Sometimes he would pray all night. His whole life
was a life of prayer. Said he, "I would not rise from my seat
without lifting my heart to God."

Martin Luther said, "If I fail to spend three hours in prayer
each morning, the devil gets the victory through the day. I
have so much business I cannot get along without spending
three hours daily in prayer." David Brainerd, the mighty

missionary to the Indians, once said, "I love to be alone in my cottage where I can spend much time in prayer."

Adoniram Judson said, "Arrange thy affairs, if possible, so that thou canst leisurely devote two hours every day, not merely to devotional exercise, but to the very act of secret prayer and communion with God . . . to be resolute in His cause. Make all practical sacrifices to maintain it."

You may not have hours to devote to prayer. D. L. Moody never spent more than fifteen minutes in prayer. But he prayed *often* and *about everything*. It is important that you have a definite time when you get alone with God every day. Not everyone can spend great periods of time. But surely there are few people, if any, who could not spend at least ten to fifteen minutes in Bible study and fifteen minutes in prayer daily.

Let me urge you to begin the day with your quiet time. I find that the more I commit myself to the Lord in the morning the less I have to confess to Him at night. We need food to strengthen us for the physical demands of our daily routine. Matthew 4:4 and 1 Peter 2:2 indicate that the Word of God is spiritual food.

> . . . It is written, Man shall not live by bread alone, but by every word that proceedeth out of the mouth of God.
>
> (Matthew 4:4)

> As new born babes, desire the sincere milk of the word, that ye may grow thereby. (1 Peter 2:2)

If you would be strong, you must have spiritual food at the beginning of the day to sustain you through it. You are not likely to suffer great temptations while you are sleeping. The great strains and stresses will be encountered during the day. Of course it is well to spend some time with the Lord before going to bed at night. But let me urgently suggest that you make your personal devotions a matter of first concern in the morning. An old professor of mine had the motto, "No Bible, no breakfast. Speak to no one until you have spoken to God."

The effectiveness of your brief moments of prayer will be

contingent upon these periods spent in prayer. Don't say you have no time. Some may have more money than others. Some may have more talent than others. But we are all on an even footing when it comes to time. We each have sixty seconds to each minute, sixty minutes to each hour, twenty-four hours to each day, seven days to each week, fifty-two weeks to each year.

As an evangelist, I am gone from home a great deal. There are occasions when on my way from one city to another I can stop at my home for a few minutes. It is a delight of my heart, and my wife and son give evidence that this delight is reciprocated. Suppose, however, that when I have a week off between meetings I refused to go home. Suppose I would go off to visit some friends instead. The next time I "bounced in" I would probably "bounce out" just as fast. My family knows I love to be at home and that I spend every possible moment at home. This knowledge makes even the briefest visits enjoyable to all of us.

So, too, our brief visits with the Lord bring mutual rejoicing if we are faithful in setting aside larger segments of time to commune with Him in deliberate and earnest intercession. Then "would our hearts condemn us not."

When to pray? Let us once again paraphrase Philippians 4:6, and hear — "Let your requests be made known *perpetually* unto God."

Remember, perpetual prayer is the answer to perpetual care.

24

For What to Pray

Be careful for nothing; but in *everything* by prayer and supplication with thanksgiving let your requests be made known unto God. (Philippians 4:6)

Casting all your care upon him; for he careth for you. (1 Peter 5:7)

Since you worry about everything, pray about everything. "In *everything* by prayer and supplication with thanksgiving let your requests be made known unto God." Peter tells us to cast *all* our care upon Him. Turn *every* care into a prayer.

You may pray about the smallest thing and about the greatest thing. Set no boundaries with respect to God's care. It is a wide open field. You may pray for the fullness of the Holy Spirit. You may also pray for a new pair of shoes. Go to God about the food you eat, the water you drink, the clothing you wear.

Nothing is too small for Him to notice. Does He not attend the funeral of every sparrow? Has He not numbered the hairs of your head? Even the things you might consider big are little in comparison with Him. Our entire earth is like a mere speck of sand on the beach of the great universe. If God is willing to consider this little speck He would just as well stoop a little lower and consider our smallest problems.

You worry about the smallest things, do you not? Well, pray about the smallest things, since prayer is God's antidote to worry.

Read it again: "Casting *all* your care upon him, for he careth for you." The words translated care here are two distinct and different words in the original. The word *care* used in the first instance is the same word translated "anxious." It refers to the same word relating to worry, "to divide the mind." The word *care* used in the second instance refers to God's solicitous interest in our highest good. Cast *all* your mind dividers, mind distracters, worries on Him for He is solicitous of your highest good. Cast them *all* on Him.

You know the old song by Tindley, "Take Your Burden to the Lord and Leave It There." The chorus goes,

> Leave it there, leave it there.
> Take your burden to the Lord and leave it there.
> If you trust and never doubt,
> He will surely lead you out.
> Take your burden to the Lord and leave it there.

The trouble with us is we pretend to take our burdens to the Lord, but we don't leave them with Him. We bring them back again.

Close friends of our family were living in Darlington, Maryland, in the early forties. The husband and father was a classmate of my father during their school days. They had eight children. The mother, whom we affectionately called "Aunt Edith," was coming home from a neighbor's house one Saturday afternoon. As she came nearer she saw five of her youngest children huddled together in great concentration of interest and effort. As she came near, all the time trying to discover the center of attraction, she was aghast to see them playing with baby skunks. She screamed at the top of her voice, "Children, run!" *Each one grabbed a skunk and ran!* Isn't that what we often do? We have our little worries, our little problems — our little skunks. We take them to the Lord in prayer. He says, "Run." Instead of leaving them there, we grab the stinking little things and run.

No problem that I as a Christian have is too great or too insignificant for God's loving care. This is a thrilling thought that you will do well to ponder again and again.

A. T. Pierson, Bible teacher extraordinary, sat one day with George Muëller, the great Englishman of faith. Mr. Muëller was relating to Dr. Pierson some of the marvelous things God had done for the Faith Orphanage at Bristol. As Mr. Muëller talked he wrote, and Dr. Pierson noticed he was having difficulty with his pen point. In the midst of the conversation, Mr. Muëller seemed oblivious to the visitor. He bowed his head for a moment or two in prayer and then began writing again. Dr. Pierson said, "Mr. Muëller, what were you praying about just now?"

"Oh," said Mr. Muëller, "perhaps you didn't notice that I was having trouble with this pen point. I haven't another and this is an important letter, so I was asking the Lord to help me so that I could write it clearly."

"Dear me," said Dr. Pierson, "a man who trusts God for millions of pounds also prays about a scratchy pen point."

If Mr. Muëller had been like many of us, he would have become hot and bothered. Possibly he would have become a little exasperated with the man who sold him the pen or the company that made the pen. Perhaps he would have indulged in morbid reflection wondering why he didn't buy a pen of another make instead of the miserable pen that was giving him trouble. Or, if he had been like many of us he may have in disgust thrown the pen down and discontinued the writing of the letter, with the result that his conscience would have bothered him later on for not having written. This would have added to the stress and anxiety. I draw your attention to this because I think it is one of the most lucid examples of the power of prayer in the seeming trivia of life.

Some there are who think we should pray only for problems of great magnitude. They consider it an insult to God and a waste of His time to pray for the so-called small things. It is here that we need the faith of a little child.

One day, many years ago, my father was replacing a burned-out bulb in the taillight of our old car. In replacing the lens he noticed he had lost a little screw in the tall grass. He had an urgent appointment for that night and not much time to spare. He searched and searched for the little screw, but to no avail. My younger brother Tom, then five or six years old, was playing next door with a friend. Finally, Dad called Tom and his friend over to contribute their help in finding the insignificant but essential little screw. When Dad told the children what he wanted Tom said, "Dad, have you prayed about it?"

My father replied, "No, I haven't, Tom."

Tom said, "Well, let's pray, Daddy." Tom prayed and said in substance, "Heavenly Father, Daddy has lost the screw that he needs for the taillight of his car. He can't find it and he needs it badly. Help us to find it. Thank You, Jesus. Amen."

Believe it or not, as soon as Tom had finished his prayer — so illustrative of the childlike faith that honors God — Dad put his hand down in the tall grass and retrieved the screw. Coincidence? Not at all! It was a distinct answer to prayer.

Possibly you read some years ago the article in *Reader's Digest* telling about the circumstances leading to Billy Graham's going on the air coast to coast. Many people had been after him to secure a coast-to-coast weekly broadcast. He had hesitated, saying that there were many other fine coast-to-coast broadcasts of the Gospel. Also the finances were not available.

An increasing number of people insisted that for the glory of God and the profit of the people of America individually, as well as for America as a nation, it was imperative that Billy go on the air. Did Graham fret and stew and worry about whether or not he ought to go on? Did he let the decision upset him and thus reduce his effectiveness for Christ? Did he vacillate between the two possibilities? No. He simply took the issue to God in prayer.

Without publicizing the fact he put out a fleece as did Gideon. He prayed that if the Lord was leading him to broadcast the Gospel coast-to-coast each week He would provide $25,000 within a specified time. As I recall, by the morning of the final day a little more than $23,000 had come in. Dr. Graham had set $25,000 as the figure. Did the fact that $25,000 in full had not come in upset him? Did he say, "Well, this is close enough"? Did he say, "My prayer is answered"? No. He had made his appeal to the Lord. He was honestly trying to know the will of God. His whole interest was the glory of God. If $24,995 had come in, Dr. Graham would not have gone on the radio. Before the day was over, however, the full $25,000 had come in and he knew the direction in which God was leading him.

Some of you say, "But really, some of the things that come to my mind are too insignificant to pray about." Do you really believe that? If you believe they are too insignificant to pray about, then why do you not believe they are too insignificant to worry about? Put this down. Anything big enough to worry about is big enough for you to pray about. Philippians 4:6 tells us in substance, "Don't worry about *anything* whatever; but in *everything* let your requests be made known unto God."

In this book is set down the biblical formula for victory over worry. If you are to have victory in putting this formula in operation, it is mandatory that you enlist the strength of Almighty God.

In your prayer ask God for the grace to enable you to rejoice, to control your feelings, regulating them according to His will, to count your many blessings. Ask Him to give you grace to respond to ingratitude with serenity. Call upon Him for the grace of becoming genuinely interested in other people.

By prayer call upon God to help you live in the consciousness of His nearness and therefore to display that poise which is the hallmark of the domination of the infinite God in the life of finite man.

Through prayer ask God to give you grace to "gird up the loins of your mind" so that you might have the mind of Christ.

Let this mind be in you, which was also in Christ Jesus.
(Philippians 2:5)

Through prayer you will enlist divine help in the matter of self-control, in the matter of relaxation (resting in the Lord) in the matter of enthusiasm, in the matter of scheduling your day's activities, in the matter of your hobbies and sidelines, in the matter of living each day to the full by "redeeming the time," in the matter of the development of skill, in the matter of industry.

Through prayer spend time with God until you know His mind and do His will in the all-important matter of stewardship. Through the right kind of prayer life you will be strengthened to live the surrendered life so essential to the poise which conquers worry.

Through prayer you can duplicate the request of earnest men many years ago who, turning to Jesus said, "Teach us to pray."

The direct answers of God in response to your prayer give you strength to battle and conquer this vicious sin of worry. Apart from the blessings of prayer itself there is also a therapeutic value in the actual time and quiet spent before God.

Pray about everything. Turn every care into a prayer and *win over worry*.

Part 5

Peace

25

Perfect Peace

And the peace of God, which passeth all understanding, shall keep your hearts and minds through Christ Jesus.

(Philippians 4:7)

Ponder my translation of verse 7:

If you do this, then the peace of God, far more effective than any forethought or contrivance of man will keep watch over your hearts and your thoughts in Christ Jesus.

The word translated "peace" can also be translated "tranquillity," "harmony," "concord," "security," "safety," "prosperity," "felicity." Worry cannot survive in this kind of atmosphere. Just as worry means "divide the mind," so we might say that peace is "uniting the mind," fastening it upon worthwhile goals and stimulating it with worthwhile motives.

God is the Author of this peace. It is "the peace of God."

And God is not the Author of confusion.

For God is not the author of confusion, but of peace, as in all churches of the saints. (1 Corinthians 14:33)

He is the Author of unity.

Endeavoring to keep the unity of the Spirit in the bond of peace. (Ephesians 4:3)

This is a genuine peace begotten of God. This is not the attitude of the man who takes everything lightly — who snaps his fingers, whistles and sings. This fellow is a heedless, foolish, light-headed and light-heeled fellow who for a little while may dance and sing. He simply postpones his sorrow. The day will come when he will give account. The day will come swiftly and with a vengeance.

This peace is far different than that attitude and disposition embraced by the Stoic. The Stoic braces his nerves. He will be shaken and moved by nothing. Run a knife into him. He feels the pain, but he will not show it. Despite all manner of rough knocks and blows in the rough and tumble world he has set his teeth, and no expression will escape him to show that he feels or winces. This is not peace.

This peace is far different from that attitude and disposition embraced by the laughing Epicurean who chortles out, "Let us eat, drink, and be merry for tomorrow we die." We are not steel-nerved Stoics. We will live it up.

This peace is based upon fact. It is not a self-manufactured hallucination designed to color the facts. This peace is based upon the fact of God's all sufficiency. It is also based upon our willingness to cast ourselves in self-confessed helplessness upon Him in response to which He lives through us His own life, bringing harmony, purpose, meaning and poise to our lives.

Let me make a distinction between *peace with God* and *peace of God*. Every child of God has peace with God.

> Therefore being justified by faith, we have peace with God through our Lord Jesus Christ.   (Romans 5:1)

But not every child of God has the peace of God. No one can enjoy the peace *of* God who does not have peace *with* God. On the other hand, it is possible, as witness the experiences of multitudes of Christians, to have peace *with* God and fail to appropriate the peace *of* God.

This peace *of* God has its foundation in the fact that God doeth all things well. It has its source in the fact that Jesus "will never leave thee nor forsake thee" (Hebrews 13:5).

Do you remember the story in Mark 4 of our Lord's trip across the Sea of Galilee? He was asleep in the bottom of the boat. The winds became furious. The waves sprang higher and higher in the air. Soon a tempestuous storm was raging. The little boat was perched perilously aloft the crest one moment only to be dashed into the darksome vortex the next. The terrified disciples cried out, "Lord, save us. We perish!" Jesus was asleep! What peace.

Jesus arose and subdued the storm, and then turned to the disciples and said, "Oh, ye of little faith. Why are ye so fearful?" I can hear them muttering, "Little faith? Little faith? We are veteran seamen. We have never seen a storm like this, and you call it little faith!" Ah, yes. You see, Jesus didn't say, "Let us go out in the middle of the sea and get drowned." He said, "Let us pass over unto the other side" (Mark 4:35).

Now, dear friend, when you have invited Christ into your life and when you have turned the helm over to His control and when you have heard His words of assurance, "Thou art mine. I will never leave thee, nor forsake thee" (Hebrews 13:5), there is made available to you a peace the world cannot give and the world cannot take away.

Notice several points about the peace Christ can give:

(1) It is a peace that "passeth all understanding." This may be interpreted in two ways.

First, it may be interpreted as too great for the poor grasp of our limited concepts. It is deeper, broader, sweeter, more heavenly than the joyful Christian himself can explain. He enjoys what he cannot understand.

There is another sense in which the words *passeth all understanding* refer to superiority over human forethought or intellectual contrivance. Here is a man who has worries. He tries through the efforts of his own understanding to resolve his worries. He fails. He fails miserably. He may resort to Stoicism or Epicureanism or the power of positive thinking, but he fails.

This man comes to God's Word. He responds affirmatively to God's commands. Having entered into peace *with*

God he now utilizes that formula which gives the peace of God: Praise, Poise and Prayer. *Perfect peace is his privileged possession.* In this sense it passes understanding, in that it far exceeds in effectiveness all human contrivance and forethought.

(2) This peace is indestructible. It "shall keep your hearts and minds through Christ Jesus." Paul here brings into union the conceptions of peace and of war, for he employs a distinctly military word to express the office of this divine peace. That word, translated "shall keep," is the same as the word translated in another of his letters, "kept . . . with a garrison" (2 Corinthians 11:32).

This peace of God takes upon itself militarylike functions. It garrisons the heart and mind. By *heart and mind* are not meant two different faculties, the emotional and the intellectual. Here, as is always the case in God's Word, *heart* means the whole inner man whether considered as thinking, willing, purposing, or effectuating any other inward and volitional functions. The word *mind* does not mean another part of man's nature. Rather if refers to the total products of the operations of the heart. The revised version renders it "thoughts" and that is correct if it be made to include emotions, affections and purposes as well as thoughts in the more restricted sense. The peace of God garrisons and guards the whole man in the full scope of his manifold operations. This divine peace can be enjoyed in the midst of warfare.

This is an indestructible peace that guards and garrisons one against all care, anxiety, change, suffering and conflict. It gives unalterable rest in God.

Deep in the bosom of the ocean beneath the region where winds howl and billows break there is calm, but the calm is not stagnation. Each drop in the fathomless abyss may be raised to the surface by the power of the sunbeams, expanded there by their heat, and sent on some beneficent mission across the world. Even so, deep in our hearts beneath the storm, beneath the raging winds and the lashing waves this peace forms a central calm, a calm that is not stagnation. "Drops" of this calm may be raised to the surface of our behavior by the power of the Son of Righteousness — Jesus Christ, the Light of the World — expanded there by the heat of the Holy Spirit and sent on beneficent service across the world.

(3) This peace is perpetual. The tense used here is future indicative and the context makes it clear that it is the progressive future which means continuous and unabated action.

Stop perpetually worrying. Perpetually let your requests be made known unto God. And you have the assurance that perpetual peace will garrison and guard your mind and heart through Christ Jesus. What an antidote to worry!

The assurance of this peace is conditional upon no outside circumstance, for this peace is possible only through Christ. A life without Christ is the life without peace. Without Him you have excitement, worldly success, fulfilled dreams, fun, gratified passions, but *never peace!*

Christian friend, before you were saved you had no peace, did you? The Christless heart is like a troubled sea that cannot rest. There is no peace for it.

Now you are a Christian. The Lord has brought you peace with respect to your relationship with Himself and with respect to your outlook on eternity. However, if you are to enjoy the peace of God over daily worries and cares and anxieties, small though they be — "the little foxes spoil the vines" — you must fix your mind upon Him. "Looking unto Jesus" (Hebrews 12:1).

Keep your mind "stayed" on Him. This will enable you to fulfill the Bible formula of Praise, Poise and Prayer.

Here is the glorious conclusion:

PRAISE PLUS POISE PLUS PRAYER EQUALS PERFECT PEACE!

As Christ lives in you "your peace shall be as a river, and your righteousness as the waves of the sea."

Peace be with you.